The Sun Hasn't
Fallen from the Sky

ALISON GANGEL started her teaching career
as Head of Music at a comprehensive school in
Newcastle upon Tyne, and now teaches English at
a Catholic comprehensive school in Gateshead. She
has lived in Newcastle upon Tyne for over twenty
years with her daughters Lorna and Jessica. *The Sun
Hasn't Fallen from the Sky* is her first book.

The Sun Hasn't Fallen from the Sky

A MEMOIR

ALISON GANGEL

BLOOMSBURY

LONDON · BERLIN · NEW YORK · SYDNEY

Bloomsbury Publishing Plc
50 Bedford Square
London WC1B 3DP

www.bloomsbury.com

Bloomsbury Publishing, London, New York, Berlin and Sydney

A CIP catalogue record for this book is available from the British Library

ISBN 978 1 4088 2205 0

10 9 8 7 6 5 4 3 2

Typeset by Hewer Text UK Ltd, Edinburgh
Printed in Great Britain by Clays Limited, St Ives plc

For Albert

A Note to the Reader

I began writing this memoir in an effort to make sense of a chaotic childhood and its repercussions. To protect the privacy of individuals, a number of names and incidents have been changed and some people from my childhood have not been mentioned at all. As the book evolved, for the sake of a narrative arc, the odd scene was brought forward in time, small embellishments added, dialogue re-created. Despite this, everything here reflects the reality of my childhood, if not in the minute detail of conversations I couldn't possibly remember at such distance then certainly in spirit. I did very much intend, however, to pay some sort of tribute to my music teacher. Everything I've written about my early love of music – and of him – is true: my regard for him continues to be deep and heartfelt, my love and gratitude inestimable.

Alison Gangel, November 2010

PART ONE

I

Autumn, 1968

'Give that girl a spotlight,' says my da, pointing straight at me. 'C'mon, Puddin, your turn.'

I stand in front of the coal fire and hold onto the sides of my dress. My da's holding the bottle of sherry to my mouth like a microphone.

'Right, hen, whit's it gonnay be?'

'Ah'll sing "Big Spender",' I tell him.

Everyone claps. Shuggy starts the introduction: *Dah Dah-di Dah Doo-Dah.*

The minute you walked in the joint (wiggle
   wiggle)
Ah could see you were a man of disingshun (point to
   Shuggy)
A real big spender
Good lookin (point to Da)
So refined
Wouldn't you like to know what's goin on in ma mind
   (point to head)
So let me get right to the point (wiggle wiggle)
Ah don't pop ma cork for every guy I see
Hey big spender (Hey big spender)
Spee-eeee-eee-eee-nd a little time with me.

Big Isa puts her glass between her knees and sticks her fingers in her mouth to whistle. Everybody claps.

'C'mere, Puddin!' shouts my da, fiddling with his change. I stand in front of him and he pats the top of my head. 'Top-notch performance, darlin.'

I hold both hands open and he empties his hand into mine. I can see at least two threepenny bits and a shilling amongst the pennies. Shuggy drops a two-bob bit into my pile as I pass.

'Fuckin great wee singer ye've got there, Jim . . . fuckin magic.'

My da pulls my ma onto his knee while she's trying to fill Big Isa's glass and grabs her diddies from behind. Morag and I giggle.

'Did ah ever tell ye how me an yer ma met?'

My mammy puts her hand across my da's mouth but he pulls it away.

'She wis naked from the waist up,' he says, making his eyes go big. 'Gettin washed at the sink.'

Morag covers her mouth with her hand.

'She had the most beautiful diddies ah'd ever seen.' My da smiles as he rocks my mother in his arms. *You're just too good to be true*, he sings into her hair, *can't take my eyes off you*. My mammy kisses him and gets up from the chair to finish pouring Big Isa's drink.

Morag gives me a nudge. 'How much did ye get?'

'Ah don't know,' I shrug.

'D'ye want me tae count it fur ye?'

'Naw, it's awright. Ah'll count it later.'

'Jus' show is how much.'

'Ah'll show ye later,' I say, without looking at her. She elbows me in the ribs and I squeeze my hand over the money.

'Yer song wis shite,' she says, and gets up and sits at my da's feet.

'C'mon, Paddy, you're next,' says my da, patting Morag on the head. She won't budge.

'Ah'll get up,' says Isa's son Doanal. 'Ah've goat a brilliant joke.'

'Ladies and gentlemen,' says my da with the sherry bottle back at his mouth. 'I give you . . . MONKEYONI.'

Doanal pulls his hair over his ears then sticks his hands back in his pockets. 'A man walks intae the butcher's and says, "Huv ye goat a sheep's heid?" An the butcher says, "Naw, it's just the way ah comb ma hair." '

My da throws his head back and slaps his knee. Shuggy spits his drink all over the carpet and wipes the snotters from his nose. Doanal waits for a minute to see if they'll give him some money. Shuggy takes a hankie from his pocket and starts pressing it against the carpet.

'Ah'm sorry, Gina,' he says to my mammy, in between laughs. 'Ah'm really sorry.'

Doanal takes his place back on the couch. The coins start to slide in my hand. The tighter I hold them, the more they slide. I change hands and wipe the sweaty one on my dress.

'It's time they were in bed, Frankie,' says my ma. 'It's efter midnight.'

My da wipes his eyes. He still cannot speak. I can feel Morag staring at my back as we head into the kitchen. My ma turns the mattress over and straightens the sheets. The bed is part of the wall and she cannot reach the far end. While Morag takes off her clothes, I slide the coins into my sock.

'Straight tae sleep,' says my ma, tucking the blankets under our chins. She smells of hairspray and cigarettes. The light goes off and the kitchen door is shut. I lie still. I don't want Morag to hear the coins.

'Where's the money?' she asks. 'Ah'll help ye count it.'

'Ah gave it tae my ma, tae watch fur me.'

I wait for the kick. It doesn't come.

The scratching starts at the cooker and moves round to the sink. Morag pulls the blankets over our heads. Dusty Springfield and Frank Sinatra are singing in our living room.

'Choose who ye want tae live wi!' shouts my da.

He's got a poker in his hand. The light is hurting my eyes.

'If ye want tae live wi that daft cunt, yer welcome tae im!' screams my ma.

He belts her across the back with the poker. My ma grabs the frying pan off the cooker and whacks him on the side of the head. Blood gushes down his face and onto his shirt. He staggers against the kitchen door and drops the poker. My ma kicks it out of the way.

'Come near me again, ya bastard, an'll fuckin kill ye.'

She's holding on to the frying pan with both hands. I can't breathe. My arms start to shake.

'Kill me, ya hoorin cunt.'

My da says it quietly like his teeth are stuck together. He moves towards her slowly. My ma takes another swing but he catches her wrist and punches her in the face. She drops to the floor, banging her head on the edge of the cooker. My da doesn't stop. He's kicking her back and her head when Morag lets the police in.

2

It's ready. Morag sits on the pavement at one side of the old sheet and I sit at the other. She leans against the wall at the front of our house and moves the goods around. We have a Cindy doll with one leg, a pack of cards, an old lampshade, some marbles, a pen, a half-used bottle of perfume and four pink and white spongy rollers.

Mrs Fisher comes out of the close and stops to button her cardigan.

'Whit've ye goat there, lassies?'

She picks up the lampshade with tassels.

'We're huvin a jumble sale, Mrs Fisher,' says Morag. 'Ye kin buy that if ye want.'

Mrs Fisher starts to laugh and shakes her head.

'A jumble sale, eh?'

She giggles and puts the lampshade back on the sheet. She walks slowly down the street. Morag picks up the lampshade and tries to straighten out the bashes. I want to tell her that she's making it worse but I keep quiet.

'Ah'm gonnay buy ginger an Caramacs wi ma money,' says Morag, putting the lampshade back in its place. She's already had a Caramac this morning and penny caramels and a bar of nougat. She said if I lent her some of my money from last night she'd pay it back out of her half of what she makes from the jumble sale. She took most of it.

'Ah'm gonnay buy Lovehearts an Spangles an a tin a Creamola Foam.'

Morag isn't listening. She does a handstand against the wall. I like watching her face get redder and redder. The ground is hard but warm. I stretch my legs out in front of me and press the backs of them to the ground to feel the heat.

A blue car stops on the other side of the street and a man with a briefcase gets out. He looks at us before locking the car door.

'Not at school today?' he asks. We both stay silent. He kneels down and looks at our stuff. 'Is your mum in?'

Morag answers, 'Aye.' The man picks up the marbles and asks me how much. I look at Morag and she says, 'Tuppence.' The man puts the marbles in his pocket and takes out his wallet. I smile at Morag and she grins back. The man hands me two brown pennies and gives Morag the same. He gets up and goes to our front door.

We take turns to go to the shop. Morag goes first. While I'm waiting, a man with a dog walks past. It starts sniffing our things and trying to get its nose under my dress. The man pulls at its leash, hard. They carry on walking. I sort the rollers and the lampshade back into place and use the sleeve of my cardigan to rub the wetness from the dog's nose off my leg. Morag calls into the house for a drink.

'Awright, Shuggy,' shouts the man with the dog. I look up and Shuggy gives the man a wave. His hand goes back into his pocket and he walks quickly towards me.

'Whit's aw this?' he says, rattling his change.

'A jumble sale. We've awready sold some marbles.'

He bends over the sheet to look at the stuff. He winks at me.

'Ah think ah'll get this perfume fur ma girlfriend.' He picks up the bottle and sniffs the lid. 'How much d'ye want fur it?'

I tell him tuppence and hope it isn't too much. He gives me a sixpence and tells me to hang onto the perfume because he'll get it later. I stick it under the corner of the sheet so that nobody else can buy it.

Morag brings a milk bottle full of water and passes it to me. She hasn't cleaned it properly. There're thick lumps of milk stuck in the grooves. I wipe it with the sleeve of my cardigan until it's mostly off and take a drink. I pass the bottle back to her and tell her about Shuggy buying the perfume.

'Much?' she asks.

'Well ah said tuppence but he gave us sixpence.'

Morag smiles. 'Ah'll go tae the shop an bring back your half,' she says, 'then you kin go.'

I grip the sixpence. She still hasn't given me the change from the last time and she still hasn't paid me back any of the money from last night.

'Why don't we wait an see if we sell anythin else? Then we kin go tae the shop the gither.'

Morag's already up on her feet. She sticks her hand out. 'Ah want ma money noo.'

I hand over the sixpence. I wish I hadn't told her about it. She bombs to the shop.

The man with the briefcase steps out of our house. My ma stands in the doorway. She looks like my doll that got squashed in the couch. One of *her* eyes was stuck as well and her hair was full of tugs. The man smiles but I don't smile back. My da says *they're a shower a cunts an they want tae stop poking their noses inty other people's business.*

'Run tae the shop, Ailsa, an get me some Askits.' My ma holds out the money. I don't really want to leave our stuff but there's no sign of Morag. I take the money and walk slowly, looking back every few steps.

Morag almost crashes into me as I turn the corner. Her cheeks are bulging. She hands me one of the bags she's holding. 'Ah jush got your sweeshts ash well.'

She pushes past me.

'Ah should huv more than this!' I shout, but she doesn't turn round. I look inside the bag. There's a caramel, a lolly and three chewing-gum balls. I scream as hard as I can.

'AH WANTED TAE BUY MA OWN SWEETS!'

Morag keeps walking.

I get my ma's Askits and take them straight back to her. There's no point in telling her about Morag. When she's like this, she cannot be bothered. I step into the house without even looking at Morag. I'm not going to talk to her or play with her ever again. And then later, when she's got no sweets left, I'm going to spend the rest of my money from the party and not give her anything and I'm going to eat everything dead slow and make it last for ages.

Shuggy's putting the lid back on a half-bottle of whisky.

'Fuck em, Gina.'

My ma pours the powder straight into her mouth. I sit on the window sill to keep an eye on Morag. If anyone stops to look at our stuff, I'll be out like a shot.

'Fuckin SS,' says Shuggy, offering my ma the bottle.

She shakes her head and sips at her tea. The only sound in the room is coming from the fire. It's making big cracking noises. The flames look like they're stretching. Shuggy flicks his ash into the coal bucket at his side.

'Fuck it,' says my ma, taking the bottle out of Shuggy's hand. She takes a couple of mouthfuls and hands him back the bottle. 'Ah'm sick ay these cunts, Shuggy. Did ye see im? Perched on the edge ay the settee, knees the gither like a wummin, aw business wi the briefcase an the forms.'

Shuggy laughs and passes her the bottle again. 'It wis the smooth wee hands ah couldny get away wi.'

My ma flicks her ash into the fire and shifts the coals

with the poker. 'Ah bet ye they'll still be too big fur his prick.'

Shuggy laughs but my ma's not laughing.

'The cunt canny stop imself, it's aw *wards of court* this an *care orders* that, but he kin talk till ma fanny rides Brando, ah'm done bein scared ay that lot, ah'm way past the greetin and the promisin tae dae better. When they've marked yer card it's fuckin marked.' My ma lights another fag and flicks it straight away, even though it doesn't need it. 'Shower a cunts the lot ay them.' My ma stares at the fire.

'That looks sore by the way.' Shuggy takes another drink from the bottle. 'Whit the fuck happened? When ah left, Frankie wis well oot the game.'

My ma shrugs her shoulders and keeps looking at the fire.

'Ah mean it's wan thing fightin, but there's nae need fur that.'

He points his head towards my ma's face. She takes a long draw of her cigarette.

'One minute it's *Ma eyes adored you* an the next it's *Boom bang a fuckin bang.*'

My ma nearly smiles.

An old man stops outside the window. He points to something on the sheet. I think it's the cards. He says something then smiles and walks away. Morag sticks her two fingers up at him.

'He's a fuckin bampot,' says Shuggy, 'an ah'll tell im that, the next time ah see im.'

My ma gets up off the chair and throws the last of her fag into the fire.

'D'ye want one?' she says, holding the mug in front of her.

'Ah'd love one,' he smiles, 'but ah suppose ah'll huv tae make do wi a cup a tea.'

My ma walks through to the kitchen. Shuggy laughs quietly to himself. Shuggy's not handsome like my da. His shoulder twitches and his face flicks to the side. The back of his neck's all hairy and he wears glasses. I think he was only kidding about having a girlfriend. Shuggy's funny. He has my ma and da in stitches.

Morag starts moving the stuff around again. I pull my head back from the window so she can't see me looking.

Shuggy gets up and lifts the lid on the record player. He takes the pile off from last night and puts them back in their covers. He turns the volume down before putting the needle on the record. Nat King Cole. 'When I Fall in Love'. Shuggy goes back to his chair and sings quietly to himself until my ma comes back with the tea.

3

My ma shouts us up for school. I think it's because that man came to the house. Morag doesn't move. I don't know if she's really sleeping or just trying to ignore my ma. I climb across her and take my pile of clothes from yesterday into the living room.

'Ah'm up, Ma.'

My ma lifts her head from under the covers.

'Morag! Get yer fuckin arse in here.'

The mattress squeaks next door. A few seconds later, Morag appears with her clothes.

'Get yersels a piece an jam before ye go, an stay away fae that fuckin cooker.'

She pulls the blankets over her head.

The woman in the school office pushes her lips together and shakes her head.

'What time do you call this? School starts at nine o'clock sharp, not ten twenty-five.'

She opens a register and uses her finger to find the Ds. 'Your mother'll be getting a letter about this.'

My ma's not bothered. She rips the letters up and throws them in the fire.

'Get off to your classes, if you can still remember where they are.' Morag opens the door that leads to the main hall. 'And make sure you apologise to your teachers ...'

Our classrooms are next to each other at the far end of the hall. Morag's teacher is dead strict. My teacher reads good stories and shows you the pictures in the books. I don't like sums but I like painting.

We chap on the doors at the same time. Miss Connor is working at her desk.

'Sorry ah'm late, Miss Connor, we slept in.'

I can hear Mrs Oliver-Trent shouting at Morag next door. *What time do you call this?*

My class is silent. Morag's class is silent.

A boy with ginger hair is sitting in the chair that I used to sit in. Miss Connor points to the seat by the window in the front row. Mrs Oliver-Trent is still shouting. *Your mother's contempt for this establishment is patently obvious.*

Miss Connor tells the rest of the class to carry on with their work. She lifts my arithmetic jotter off the shelf behind her desk. I know it's arithmetic because it's yellow. The work is on the blackboard, adds and take-aways. Miss Connor is going through the first one with me when there's more shouting from next door and our room goes silent again.

What did you say? WHAT did you call me?

Footsteps thunder across the room, a chair scrapes against the wooden floor.

Fuck off, ya ugly cunt.

Big breaths of shock are passed round my classroom. They're not really shocked. They're just sooking up to Miss Connor. I can hear the footsteps of Mrs Oliver-Trent on the main hall's wooden floor.

My ma'll kick fuck oot ay you when she hears aboot this.

The Headmaster will sort you out, young lady, no mistake.

Every head in the class is up and listening. Janice McGinley breaks the silence by putting her hand up. Miss Connor gives her a nod.

'That's terrible language isn't it, Miss?'

Miss Connor stands in front of the class and looks at Janice.

'It's not the type of behaviour we encourage at this school.'

Janice's arm shoots up again. 'She's gonnay get in loads a trouble, in't she, Miss?'

'Shut up, McGinley, ye don't know whit yer talkin aboot.'

'Now, girls, we'll have less of that and a bit more work.'

'But she'll definitely get the belt, won't she, Miss?'

'Shut the fuck up, McGinley – yer da's the biggest freak goin – walkin aboot wi the big shoe on one foot – talk aboot that why don't ye?'

Some of the class giggle, others do the big breath thing again.

'Headmaster's office now, young lady. I'll be up to have a word with him in a second.'

I hope he sends us home. I'm sick of this place.

Morag's got both her feet up on the chair outside the Headmaster's office. She smiles when she sees me coming towards her.

'Whit did they send you up fur?'

'Tellin Janice McGinley tae shut the fuck up. The wee cunt's gonnay get it when ah get a hod ay er.' I throw myself into the chair beside Morag. She starts laughing.

'Look at the state ay ye, Puddin. Yer face is bright red. Ye look like ye've been slapped.' She cannot stop laughing. 'Did they get yer wee temper up, hen?'

She puts her face up close to mine and we both laugh. The Headmaster opens his door and stands in front of us. He waits until the giggling stops.

'This is no laughing matter, let me assure you. I shall be sending for your mother immediately.'

He walks towards the main office. A minute later the woman with the register puts her coat on and leaves through the front door.

We sit for ages but there's no sign of my ma. The smell from the dinner hall is making me hungry. They make nice dinners at the school. I've had the mince and tatties three times and the sausages and onions twice. I can hear a class singing 'Heads, Shoulders, Knees and Toes'. Miss Connor taught our class that song ages ago and all the actions to go with it. I show Morag the actions but she gives up halfway through.

Morag nudges me. My ma bursts through the school doors with the woman following behind her.

'Mrs Dunn, you'll have to calm down before you speak to the Headmaster.'

'Calm doon?' My ma's shouting really loud. 'Ye get the life pestered oot ay ye tae send them tae fuckin school an when ye dae send them, they get sent straight back? Yes want tae make up yer fuckin minds.'

The Headmaster and Miss Connor appear at the same time. The woman from the office unbuttons her coat. My ma grabs a hand each and pulls us both out of the chairs. The Headmaster moves forward.

'Mrs Dunn, we'll need to have a word about your daughters' behaviour.'

My ma turns round to face them.

'A word, is it? Ah'll gi ye a word awright. Ye kin stick yer school right up yer fuckin arse, yer nothin but a shower a cunts the lot ay ye.'

My ma swings us round as she heads for the door.

'Go on, fuck off back tae yer bay windies an yer potted plants, ya bunch a hedge-trimmin BASTARDS.'

She doesn't let go of us until we're back at our house.

4

My ma's all happy because my da's back. She's trying to make out she's not that bothered but you can tell. She's definitely happy he's back. He's had a big win on the horses so my ma and me are going to get the messages up Paisley Road West. First, she gives me the money to pay back Mrs Fisher and Alec in the corner shop. I don't like it when she sends me to ask for the money but I like it when she sends me to pay them the money back. Mrs Fisher's all chuffed with the ten bob and the packet of fags, and Alec scores my ma's name off the sheet of paper he keeps down the side of the till.

When I get back from the corner shop my da pulls me up onto his knee. He keeps squeezing my cheeks and hugging me into him.

My ma's still getting ready.

'Yer the best Ailsa in the world,' he says, 'oot ay aw the Ailsas there are – an let me tell ye there's hunners an hunners – yer definitely the best.'

I give him a kiss and smooth down his eyebrows to see if it makes him even more handsome.

My ma's black eye is gone and her lip's healed up. She looks like Sophia Loren with all her make-up. She's wearing her pink cardigan buttoned up and the tight black skirt my da likes. He gives her a whistle when she comes back into the room.

'Shuggy wis right. He nipped ma heid fur a solid week aboot how much ay a daft cunt a wis an then he demented

17

me fur another week aboot whit ah needed tae dae tae win ye back.'

My ma bends over to kiss him on the lips. Her eyelashes curl like a cat's tail. 'Nay mer chances, Frankie, ah'm fuckin sick ah livin like this.'

He crosses his heart and holds his hand out so that the palm faces my ma. With his other hand he nips her bum. She straightens up and rubs at the spot.

'Morag shouldny be long, her and Doanal are up at the park. Gie her the money fur a pie at the shop an she'll be oot till yontime.'

She rolls the notes my da gave her and folds them into her purse. He's given her extra so she can buy the gold charm bracelet she's been on about for months.

It's the first shop we go to. When she tries it on she holds out her arm and gently shakes her wrist to see how the charms move. The jeweller stares at her while she stares at the bracelet.

'I'll keep it on,' she tells him, and gets the money out of her purse. She rolls both her sleeves up a little bit as we leave the shop. There are five charms altogether: a Scottie dog, a key, a Cinderella shoe, a Cinderella coach and a book with a cross on the front. The Cinderella coach is the best.

The butcher leaves what he is doing at the machine to serve my ma straight away. She looks at the meat laid out before her. Her fingers pull at her lips. I'm not sure if it's because she can't make up her mind or if it's because she wants him to see her new bracelet.

The butcher winks at me. 'What a bonny wee thing ye are,' he says. 'Mind you, if ye turn out to be half as bonny as yer mother ye'll be doin very well.'

My ma puts her head down and starts looking for

something in her bag. She tells him a pound of stew, two sirloin steaks, a ham hough, half a pound of square sausage, six slices of black pudding and half a pound of bacon. He moves to the stew and starts weighing up her order. She looks at me as if to say what a numpty. I smile and nod my head.

'Special occasion with the steak?' He keeps his eyebrows up until my ma answers.

'It's ma husband's birthday,' she tells him. He doesn't say very much after that.

Maybe it *is* my da's birthday. Maybe that's why he looks nice today and why my ma let him back in the house. She carries the bag out of the shop.

'Is it really my da's birthday, Ma?'

'Naw,' she laughs, 'no the day it's no.'

We get the pies and the rolls from the baker's and the veg and the tins from Curley's. My ma carries the veg and the tins bag; I carry the rolls and the meat.

'We'll need tae come back, Ailsa, ah've still got tae get the two ay ye some knickers an stuff an ah wis gonnay go tae Woolworth's an get yer da that new Petula Clark record he really likes.'

'Ah'll help ye, Ma, ah'll carry yer stuff.' Woolworth's has got some good toys. We're only halfway down the street when the handles of the carrier bag start to dig into my fingers; I swap them round and move the handle part nearer the front of my hand.

'Whit wis your best toy, ma, when ye were wee?'

My ma thinks about it for a minute. I shift the handles again.

'Skipping ropes. They were the best. Ah liked them because ye could play wi them yersel, ye could take turns wi a pal or if there wis a few of ye, ye could take an end each and the rest could jump in.'

I'm in the middle of thinking that skipping ropes definitely sound like a good idea when my ma stumbles forwards and almost drops her messages. Her high heel is caught in the metal grate on the road.

'Fer fucksake.'

She pulls at her foot to get the heel unstuck. I put down my bags and use both hands to pull at the heel. It's really stuck. A fair-haired man with glasses is taking my ma's bags from her with one hand and holding onto her elbow with the other.

I stand up. 'Lean on me, Ma.'

My ma puts her hand on my shoulder. The fair-haired man crouches down at my ma's feet.

'Let's have a look at this heel,' he says, pushing his glasses back up to his eyes. My ma keeps pulling at the heel with her foot but it doesn't move. The fair-haired man gets a good grip on it and pulls hard. He lets a big breath out when he stops pulling.

'Maybe if ye take yer shoe off, Ma, it'll be easier.'

My ma digs her nails into my shoulder and gives me one of her looks.

'Nearly there,' says the fair-haired man with the glasses. He gives one final pull and the heel comes out of the grate.

'Aw thanks very much,' says my ma. 'Ah always avoid these grates but we were so busy talkin aboot skippin ropes, ah didny even notice it.' She gives him a good smile.

'A pleasure,' says the fair-haired man.

He offers to carry the bags but my ma won't let him. He hands her the bags of messages and watches her walk away. I think he's checking that the heel is OK. We turn the corner and head home.

'Whit are ye playin at, Ailsa? Tellin me tae take ma shoe aff in front ay the man. Ah've a bloody big hole the size ay Partick in me nylons. Ah'd look like a right cunt wi

20

the big toe stickin oot in the middle ay the street.' I don't like it when my ma shouts at me. 'Fucksake, Ailsa.'

My ma shakes her head and keeps walking.

'When we go back oot, Ma, ah'll remember ye tae get new nylons.'

She looks at me and smiles. 'Awright, Puddin, you remind me.'

5

My da's making the soup while my ma washes the sheet. He makes a good pot of soup. The house smells of ham and lentils and leeks. My da puts bits of raw carrot into my ma's mouth. I don't like raw carrot.

'Will ah change the record, Da? Ah think it's finished.'

'Go on, Puddin, your choice, surprise us.'

I know how to work the records really good. My ma showed me. She said you cannot let your fingers touch the record one little bit or it'll spoil it and you have to make sure the record goes back in the right sleeve to stop it from getting scratches.

I rush back into the kitchen before the record starts so that I can see the look on my da's face. He hears the first bit of the introduction.

'Excellent choice, Puddin. Ah couldny've picked a better song if ah tried.'

I knew my da would like it. He loves Tom Jones. He dances at the cooker while he stirs the soup.

Just . . . help . . . your . . . self, to my lips, to my arms, just say the word and they are yours . . . My ma looks at my da and shakes her head.

Morag's missing everything. The sweeties, the skipping ropes, the records, the soup. She's missing my da dancing.

My ma wrings out the sheet. She squeezes hard and gets some of the water out. My da does it for her and it's like a waterfall. He carries it through to the living room and hangs it over the clothes horse. He lifts the whole thing and stands it in front of the fire.

'Keep an eye on it, Puddin. Tell us when it needs turnin.'

The steam leaves the sheet and twists its way up to the ceiling. I can hear my ma squealing and laughing in the kitchen. I don't want to keep an eye on the sheet.

The front door opens. It might be Morag back from Doanal's.

'Awright, Shuggy, c'mon in, son.'

Shuggy comes into the living room holding a carrier bag in each hand.

'Where d'ye want them, Jim?' My da comes in behind him.

My ma is standing at the door with her arms folded.

'We wurney gonnay huv a drink the night, Shuggy, just a bit a dinner an some telly an that.'

Shuggy looks at my da and then at my ma.

'Don't be daft, Gina, the boy's gone tae aw the trouble a gettin a carry-oot fer fucksake.'

My ma goes back into the kitchen. Dishes are getting clattered in the sink. Cupboard doors are getting slammed. My da moves the clothes horse away from the fire.

'Canny see ye, Shuggy, fur the bloody sheet.'

'Look, Frankie, ah kin catch ye later doon the Hamilton if ye want tae get a bit a dinner an that.' He points with his head to the door. He's talking about my ma.

'Fuckin behave yersel, Shuggy, yer huvin a bit a dinner an stayin fur a drink. Fucksake, ye know yer mair than welcome in ma hoose.'

6

The police took my da away again last night. He got the big knife out and tried to stab Shuggy because he was singing that Elvis Presley song to my ma. 'Can't Help Falling in Love' . . . that one.

'D'ye take me fur some kind a mug, Shuggy?' my da started shouting at him. 'Eh? Tryin tae take the cunt oot ay me? Eh?'

Shuggy stopped singing straight away.

'Fer fucksake, Frankie, ye've got tae be kiddin. Ah'm only enjoyin the song.'

My ma got up and tried to take the knife out of my da's hand.

'Fuckin big shot, eh? Invitin people roon then no lettin the cunts enjoy themselves.'

My da shoved her back down on the couch. Shuggy jumped up to help her but my da headbutted him straight back into his chair and put the knife at his throat. My ma got out the door while he was shouting at Shuggy, 'Ye ever sing like that tae her again an ah'll cut yer fuckin balls aff. D'ye hear me?'

Shuggy nodded. 'Ah'm sorry, Frankie, fer fucksake it wis only a song.'

My da started shouting the odds again. 'Don't come inty ma hoose an try an make a cunt ooty me, Shuggy. Ah don't care if it wis only a song, it wis the way ye wer lookin at her. D'ye think ah'm stupid?'

My da straightened himself up and went back to his chair. Shuggy sat up properly and pulled the cuffs down on his shirt. My da started crying.

'Ye don't know whit it's like, Shuggy. She's gonnay go aff wi somebody else, ah know it, ah just know it.'

That was when the police came in and got the knife off my da. Shuggy was shouting at them to take it easy and was trying to pull at the policeman who had my da's arm twisted up his back. They both got put in the van. Morag and Doanal were coming out of the chip shop when they saw the police van pull away from our house. My ma locked the front door and put the big snib on. She kept calling my da names under her breath, *useless cunt . . . fuckin arsehole*.

The sheet for the bed was still damp so my ma let me and Morag sleep with her.

7

My da's banging at the front door.

'C'mon, Gina, ah'm really sorry. McAllister's lent me his car. We kin go oot fur the day an huv a picnic an that.'

My ma doesn't move. She flicks the ash from her fag into the fire.

'The wains'll love it, Gina.'

Me and Morag are up at the window. My da winks at me.

'D'ye want tae go in the car, Puddin? Loch Lomond, eh?'

He starts singing really loud, *Fur me an ma true love will never meet again on the bonny, bonny, banks of Loch Lomond.*

My ma's smiling and shaking her head. She drinks her tea and finishes her fag. My da's a good singer. Morag waves at him through the window.

'Kin we go, Ma? Kin we go wi ma da tae Loch Lomond?'

'Go on, Puddin, open the door, let the daft cunt in.'

Morag beats me to it.

'Mornin, ladies . . .' says my da, and picks us up, one in each arm. 'Your carriage awaits.'

My ma doesn't look at him when he comes into the living room. He sets us both down on the couch.

'Ah'm sorry, Gina, makin a right cunt ay masel. Ah shouldny've let Shuggy come in wi the carry-oot. We were huvin a good night up until then.'

My ma lights up another fag and offers one to my da.

'Ah did try tae tell ye but it wis aw *Ye know yer always welcome in ma hoose, Shuggy*.' My ma puts on a stupid voice when she says it. My da starts laughing.

'Pack it in, Gina, ah'm fuckin mortified.'

My ma gets a fit of the giggles and can't stop laughing. She's making us all laugh. Eventually, she gets the words out.

'The poor cunt didny know if he wis comin or goin.'

Tears are running down my da's face. My ma can hardly get her breath for laughing.

'If that wis his welcome . . .'

They take ages to stop laughing. My da wipes the tears from his eyes.

'C'mon, hen, get dressed. We'll take the wains oot fur the day.'

My ma goes in the big press and gets the clothes out for me and Morag.

'Race ye,' says Morag, pulling on her socks. My fingers start going stupid. She hasn't got any buttons on her dress but mine's got three. My da goes into the kitchen to make up some rolls and ham. Morag's got her pants on and is pulling her dress over her head.

'Where's the rolls, Gina? Huv ye no been tae the shop?'

'We need some fags an milk as well.'

By the time my da comes back from the shop we're ready. Morag won. My ma's nearly ready, she's just finishing her make-up. We help my da with the rolls and ham. He's bought biscuits and ginger and everything.

The car's a dark-green colour. Me and Morag get in the back. My da looks at me through the mirror. 'All sorted, ladies?'

I nod and look out the window. There's nobody around to see us in the car. Mrs Fisher's curtains are still closed and there's nobody coming out of the corner shop.

My da's a good driver. My ma lights up fags and passes them to him. He keeps his eyes on the road. Morag's really quiet. She puts her head back and closes her eyes.

'Whit's up?' I ask but she doesn't answer.

My ma looks at the hills and the fields. My da flicks his ash out of the small window beside the driver's wheel. It takes a long time to get to Loch Lomond. My da plays I spy but Morag doesn't want to play.

'Ah feel sick, Ma.'

My ma shifts round in her seat to look at her. 'Ah'll open the windy, hen, gi ye a bit a fresh air.'

Morag moves nearer my ma's window. The wind blows her hair straight back.

'It'll no be long noo, Morag, we're nearly there.'

Morag goes a funny colour and starts bolking.

'Ma, she's gonnay be sick, she's bolkin in the back.'

'Pull in, Frankie, we canny huv er stinkin oot the car.'

Morag puts her hand to her mouth. She's still bolking. The car stops just in time. My ma pats her back while she's being sick then comes back to the car to get a hankie out of her bag.

I move to the middle of the back seat and sit forward.

My da lights another fag.

'You awright, Puddin? Ye don't feel sick?'

'Ah'm awright, Da.'

'Great stuff, hen.'

He carries on smoking his fag. Morag's eyes are all watery when she gets back to the car. My ma dabs her eyes with the hankie. 'Sit in the front, hen, ye don't get sick if ye sit in the front, an keep the windy open a wee bit.'

My ma gets in the back seat beside me. Morag sits in the front and winds the window down a little bit. The car starts up again and we're soon on the road. My da pats Morag's knee.

We're only driving for a little while longer when my da says, 'There we are, girls, Loch Lomond.'

It looks like a picture you buy in the shops. The water isn't blue; it's a grey, blacky colour.

'Kin we go in the water, Da? Kin we go on a boat?'

Morag's feeling better. My da parks the car beside some shops. My ma's desperate for a cup of tea. I take my ma's hand; Morag takes my da's. The shops look different to the ones in Glasgow. Up here, they're painted a nice colour and the signs above them are clean and not broken. Fishing nets and buckets hang outside a shop in front of us.

'C'mon,' says my da.

We follow him inside. My ma waits outside to finish her cigarette. Morag picks the red net and bucket set. I choose the yellow. My da buys a postcard and sticks it in his pocket.

'D'ye think we'll catch some fish, Da?' Morag's swinging her bucket.

'Course ye will, hen.'

'D'ye think they'll fit in this net, Da?'

'Definentely.'

My ma points to the café on the other side of the street. The only table that's free is the small one in the window. My da tries to squeeze himself into the chair without making too much noise. My ma's shoulders start going and her hand is up at her mouth. My da smiles. He knows she's laughing at him but he doesn't look at her. They order two teas and we get some ginger. Morag wants to have a sword fight with the fishing nets but I don't want mine to get broken.

'Ma, tell er, she's gonnay break it.'

Morag kicks me under the table.

'Pack it in, the pair ay ye.'

We finish in the café and head down towards the water. There's four boats on the water.

'That's mine,' says Morag, pointing to the biggest one.

I kid on I cannot see it. She keeps pointing.

'The blue one wi the big sails up.'

I put my hand up to my eyes.

'Ye must be blind, Puddin, if ye canny see that boat, it's right there, the big one.'

'Aw that one,' I say, and start to take my shoes and socks off. My da's already paddling in the water. His trousers are rolled up to his knees. Morag's right behind him. She swishes her net around in the water like she's stirring soup.

'No like that, Paddy, nice an gentle or ye'll frighten the fish away.'

I paddle out to where they are. My ma sits on the grass on my da's spread-out coat. She's eating a roll and ham and looking at the people around her. Morag gets fed up and gives my da her fishing net and empties the bucket of water.

'Ah'm gonnay fill this up wi stones,' she says, and heads back to dry land.

It doesn't take long before Morag's bucket is full.

'Me an Ailsa'll huv a competition, Da, tae see who kin throw the stones the furthest an you kin be the judge.'

We walk back to where Morag is. She empties half her bucket of stones into my bucket. My da takes the nets and goes up to sit beside my ma.

'But you're the judge, Da, ye huv tae come back doon here.'

'Naw yer awright, Paddy, ah kin see better fae up here.'

My da takes the rest of my ma's fag and smokes it. I pick out a nice stone and hold it up to show them. They both start laughing. My da gives me the thumbs-up.

Morag takes a big long run and throws her stone really hard. I copy her but mine doesn't seem to go as far. We both look at my da.

'One tae Paddy.'

Morag's busy getting her next stone. She throws it far but not as far as the last time. I don't run this time. I just throw it as hard as I can.

'One tae Puddin.'

Morag stares at my da. Her eyebrows are nearly touching in the middle.

'She just beat ye by that much, Paddy.'

He's holding his hand up with the thumb and the next finger nearly touching.

I look for a stone that's the same as the last one. It was nearly flat and jet-black. Morag runs up to the edge of the water again and throws her hardest. Mine isn't very good.

'Two–one tae Paddy.'

I don't really like this game. Morag's definitely better at throwing than me. She rubs the stone down the side of her dress before taking her big run. It goes really far. I rub my stone down the side of my dress. My ma and da are really laughing.

'C'mon, Puddin,' they shout, 'throw yer hardest.'

I throw it as hard as I can. We both look at my da.

'Twos each.'

Morag drops her stone and marches up to where they're sitting.

'Yer kiddin, Da, her throw wis rubbish.'

They cannot stop laughing.

Morag kicks at the grass then turns to look at the water. 'Ye canny see fuck all fae up here.'

My da tries to say we'll have less of the swearing but he cannot speak. Morag's not listening anyway. She walks back down to where her bucket is and tips the lot into the water. She stays in a right huff for ages, right up until we're walking back to the car.

'Hands up if yer happy,' says my da.

I put my hand up; my ma puts her hand up. Morag doesn't.

'Cos ye know Loch Lomond's famous fur its ice cream an it's the tradition tae get happy people an ice cream before they leave so that they'll stay happy but ah'm no sure whit flavour tae get – chocolate, strawberry or vanilla … We'll sort that oot later, how many wis it again?'

My da points as he counts, one – two – three.

8

Big Isa's been at our house for the last two days, making cups of tea for my ma and sending me to the shop for rolls. My ma's stayed in her underskirt and cardigan. She keeps being sick. I think it's Big Isa's tea and all the fags they're smoking. My da hasn't been back since he dropped off McAllister's car. My ma keeps crying.

'This is the last fuckin thing ah need, Isa.'

Big Isa's reading the card my da sent to my ma from Loch Lomond, *To the real beauty of Scotland*. She smiles and puts it back on the mantelpiece.

'He's a charmer, Gina, there's nae doubt aboot that.'

My ma doesn't look up from where she's sitting.

'But where's the cunt when ye need im, Isa? This is whit ah'm talkin aboot . . . ye canny rely on im fur nothin.'

My ma starts crying again. She uses the back of her hand to wipe her eyes.

'Y'know Frankie, Gina. He has these mad benders then he's good as gold fur ages.'

'Ah'm no huvin it, Isa, ah kin tell ye now, there's no way on God's earth ah'm huvin it.'

'They bring their ain joy, Gina.'

Big Isa opens her purse and hands me sixpence.

'Go oot an play, Puddin. Morag an Doanal'll be back in a minute.'

Morag and Doanal went out this morning and they still haven't come back. I'll go to the shop then sit at my door for a while. If my da comes up the street I'll spot him straight away and run in to tell my ma.

9

Woolworth's is easy but it's still scary. We stop for breath outside a post office. Nobody has followed. The sweets pressed against my chest are squashed and the chocolate has melted in my hands. Morag pulls the bottom of her jumper forward. It's full of raspberry ruffles, orange creams, macaroons and fruit jellies.

Doanal takes a toffee penny from his pocket and pops it into his mouth. He checks the street again. 'C'moan,' he says. 'It's aw clear.'

Morag ignores him and walks into the post office. 'Huv ye goat any plastic bags, Mrs?' she asks the woman behind the counter. Morag pulls open the bottom of her jumper and shows the lady her sweets. I hold out both hands and show her mine.

'Let's have a look,' she says, bending down to look underneath. 'I saw some yesterday . . .'

Morag nudges Doanal. A small roll of notes lies beside the woman's hand. I know what they are going to do. My legs go weak and my sweets drop to the floor. Morag snatches the money and they run.

I follow them, as the woman stands up with a bag in her hand. Morag's green jumper zigzags down the street. I want to cry. They're faster than me. I'm always at the back. The jumper disappears into a close. I keep my eyes fixed on the spot.

Doanal's coughing and spitting when I find them out the back. Morag rolls the elastic band off the money. 'Whit are ye greetin fur?' she asks, straightening out the notes.

'Fuck off hame if yer gonnay start,' says Doanal, staring at the money.

Morag counts the notes into his hands. 'Eight, nine, ten.' Her hands are shaking.

Doanal starts jumping up and down.

'Ah'm gonnay get new claes an some shoes an a fitba,' he says, waving the money above his head. Morag takes the notes and stuffs them down her pants.

'Ah'll get a dress an a hairband.' She leads the way out of the close. As we cross the bridge into the city centre, I think about dresses and shoes and long white socks.

'Ah think ah should hold the money,' says Doanal. 'Ah'm the eldest an ah kin just say that ma ma sent me oot tae get ye some gear.' Morag doesn't say anything but I can tell that she's thinking about it.

'Ah'm ten an you're only eight an she's seven,' he says. 'Ah should be in charge ay the money.'

The skin at the top of my legs is rubbing together. It stings. I try keeping them apart but it slows me down and makes me walk funny. I push my skirt between my legs and it helps until the material works its way out again. Morag grabs my hand as we cross into Argyll Street then lets go to push open the doors of a café on the corner. I'm glad we're stopping. I take my seat and let my legs fall apart. Morag sorts the money out under the table and hands it to Doanal.

The man at the till comes over to our table. He's got a pen and a notepad in his hand. 'What can I get you?'

Morag and Doanal order pie, chips and beans. I ask for a roll and sausage.

'We'll huv three Irn-Brus as well,' says Morag.

Doanal hands over a pound note. The man brings the change back with the drinks.

'Kin ah get a dolly?' I say, taking a sip of Irn-Bru. 'The wan wi the bottle an the dummy an the pink nightie.'

'We'll see,' says Morag, looking round for her food.

'It wets itself efter its bottle,' I add, making sure she knows the one I mean.

'Ye better call it Puddin then,' says Doanal and they both laugh.

Morag leans back to let the man put her plate down. It looks lovely. I wish I'd got that. She pours tomato sauce all over the plate. I take a bite of my roll but the sausage is red hot. I move it around my mouth and take another sip of Irn-Bru. Doanal's halfway through his dinner already. Morag's looking at the pictures of food on the walls.

'Ah think you kin run faster than a car,' I tell Morag.

She smiles and I can see broken bits of pie at the side of her mouth.

'Ah think you're the fastest runner ah've ever seen.'

She cuts another piece of pie and dips it into her beans.

'D'ye want wannay them?' she asks, pointing with her fork to a picture on the wall. It's a banana split, with wafers, cream and a cherry on the top. I nod my head and eat the rest of my roll quickly before she changes her mind.

IO

'Remember,' says Morag, slowing down as we get to the corner of our street, 'wi found a wallet ootside the bank on Albion Street.'

She looks nice in her tartan dress and white cardigan. Doanal runs across the road to get to his own house.

'Make sure you tell Big Isa the same,' she says.

'Nae bother,' says Doanal. 'She swallys any auld shite.'

He sticks his hands in the pockets of his new jeans and disappears up the close. My arms are sore. The dolly's heavier than I thought she'd be. Her name's Angelina and she's got long eyelashes and a pink hairband. She doesn't wet herself but she cries if you tip her forward.

The lights are off in our house and the front door is locked.

'She might be up at the shop, Morag.'

Morag looks up and down the street. 'She would've left the lights on if she wis only nippin tae the shop.'

'Maybe she's up at Big Isa's.'

I hope she is. Big Isa lets you make toast and tea while her and my ma have a wee drink. She lets you choose the records as well. Morag pulls herself up to the ledge of the living-room window and cups her hands round her face. I sit Angelina on the front step and do the same on the kitchen window. I do it carefully; I don't want to scrape my new shoes.

'There's naebody in,' says Morag, wiping the dirt off her knees. The kitchen is beginning to take shape. I can just make out the edges of the bed, the kitchen sink and the cooker. The oven door is open and there's something on the floor beside it. It looks like a blanket.

'There's somethin on the floor,' I say, without taking my hands away from my face. I know if I do, it'll take ages for my eyes to get used to the dark again.

'Whit d'ye mean?' says Morag, climbing up beside me. She pushes against me and I almost lose my balance. Her face is pressed against the windowpane. My eyes find the shape quickly.

'Ah canny see anythin . . . where is it?'

'Beside the cooker . . . on the floor.'

The street's really quiet, but somebody's playing Dean Martin.

'It's my ma,' I say to Morag. 'Ah kin see the back of her head an the collar of her blouse.'

Morag jumps down onto the pavement and runs across the road to the warehouse. The men that work there sometimes give us their empty ginger bottles.

'Ma, it's me, wake up.' I bang on the window.

She doesn't move. Morag's shouting at a couple of workmen and pointing to our house. They follow her across the road.

'Ma, we've goat new claes.' I bang on the window but she doesn't hear me. 'Ah've got a new dolly, Ma . . .'

Morag pulls me off the ledge.

'Ah think she's drunk, Morag . . . an fell asleep.'

The tallest workman looks through the kitchen window. The other one bangs at the front door. Morag's watching them, wrapping the bottom of her cardigan round and round her hands. They aren't listening to me. The men break the door down and a thick, heavy smell comes out of our house.

'Go and get help,' shouts the smaller one and they both disappear through the door.

We run all the way to Big Isa's.

The policemen's coats swish really loud when they move around the room. It's freezing. They've opened all the windows and left the front door open. My ma is lying on the bed. She's really pale and her eyes are closed. Big Isa is talking quietly to a policewoman who is kneeling down in front of her. She is reading a letter and crying. The walkie-talkies crackle above our heads. I can't make out what they say. My mother's feet are sticking out from under the blanket. They're dirty.

'Did she seem depressed, Mrs Mullen . . . unhappy?'

Big Isa blows her nose and clears her throat. 'No really,' she says. 'As a matter of fact, she wis gonnay ask aboot a job at the Co-op efter she goat back fae gettin her messages in. She looked smart an tidy . . . said she'd call intae mine aboot teatime.'

Big Isa sniffs and finds a clean bit of her handkerchief. The ambulance men come in with a stretcher. One of them leans over my mother and pulls up her eyelids, then feels her wrist.

'We'll take her to the Royal . . . It's quicker.'

They lift her onto the stretcher and carry her out to the ambulance. Big Isa goes with her. I can hear Mrs Fisher at the front step. *It's a bloody shame, it is . . . that poor lassie.*

The policewoman makes a pot of tea and some pieces and jam. The taller policeman folds up the bed-settee, the shorter one lights the fire.

'She'll be awright,' he says, taking the matches from the mantelpiece.

Morag wipes her eyes with the sleeve of her cardigan. I dig my thumbnail into the palm of my hand.

'A couple of days in hospital an she'll be as right as rain.'

The policeman has made a good fire. My ma would've liked it. She would've stood with her back to it and lifted her skirt. She would've rubbed her arse a few times and winked at whoever was watching. I always winked back when she winked at me.

The front door goes and the policewoman gets up to answer it. A young woman holding a brown folder comes into the living room. She's got Angelina in her other hand.

'My name's Miss McIntyre,' she says.

My dolly's arm is flattened and her hairband's manky.

The policeman offers the social worker another cup of tea.

'No thanks,' she says. 'The car's on its way.'

He smiles and takes the empty cups through to the kitchen. She's sitting in my ma's chair. Her earrings are big and dangly. They keep getting caught in her long curly hair. She's wearing a light-brown coat with fur round the edges. My ma wanted a coat like that.

She says we won't need to stay for long, just till my ma gets better. She says we'll make lots of new friends because hundreds of children live there. She says it's got a church and a school and a swing park and a swimming pool. She smiles and makes her eyes go big as if to say so what do you think of that then?

I think they should leave us alone. I think it sounds horrible. I think they should tell my da what's happened and he'll come and get us.

'We kin stay at Big Isa's,' says Morag. 'We kin sleep on the couch.' The social worker shakes her head before Morag's finished what she's saying.

'I'm afraid Mrs Mullen wouldn't be a suitable replacement for your mum at the moment.' The policeman comes in from the kitchen.

'It's here,' he says, and starts turning off lamps and unplugging the telly. We follow the social worker out onto the street.

Mrs Fisher is standing at the close. Her arms are folded. She hasn't got her teeth in.

'It's a bloody liberty,' she says, 'takin the lassie's wains away.'

It's a big car, black and shiny. The driver holds the back door open and we climb in. The social worker pulls out a fold-out seat and sits opposite. Mrs Fisher waves as the car pulls away but I don't want to wave back.

Morag pulls at some skin on her finger. The social worker is looking for something in her bag. I think about the man lifting my mother off the floor and the way her mouth hung open until he laid her down on the bed. The tears are hot. My throat hurts. It's hard to breathe. The social worker sits forwards and puts one hand on Morag's arm and the other on mine.

'I'm sorry that this is happening to you,' she says, looking straight at us. She doesn't blink. 'None of this is your fault.'

I think about the money we stole. She grips my arm tightly.

'Your mummy loves you very much. She just needs a bit of looking after at the moment.'

Morag shakes her off. The social worker sits back in her seat and stares out of the window. I wish I could give the money back.

It's mostly sky I can see from the windows. All the buildings have gone. Morag's finger starts to bleed but it doesn't stop her. She wipes the blood on her coat and starts picking again. The social worker points at the window, an airport and some aeroplanes. She twists her head to look at one coming in to land. Fields and trees seem to go on for ever.

'Where's ma da?' asks Morag. 'If ye go an get him then he kin watch us till ma ma gets better.'

The social worker clears her throat.

'I'm afraid that won't be possible, girls.' She moves forward in her seat.

'Your dad has been sent to prison for a little while because he took some things from a warehouse that didn't belong to him.'

Morag pulls her knees up in front of her and hides her face. Her body is shaking.

'Ah want tae go back,' I tell her. 'Ah want ma mammy an ah want tae go back.'

The social worker wipes the tears from my eyes with her thumb and strokes Morag's head with her other hand.

'Will ye fuck aff!' screams Morag. 'Get yer fuckin paws aff.'

Part Two

13

The car slows down as it goes through a wide stone entrance. I think this is it. There's a big sign but I don't know what it says. I ask the social worker.

'William McGregor's Orphan Homes of Scotland.' Her voice is quiet. We stop outside the building nearest the gate. The social worker gets out. There are lots of trees and grass and flowers. Everything is green. There are words made with pink and white flowers in a circle on the grass. I ask Morag what it says. She sits forward in her seat and looks out of the window.

'Have faith in God.'

The social worker gets back in the car and gives the driver directions. The car moves slowly along neat paths. There are lots of houses standing on their own. They look like stone islands in green seas. Children stop playing and stare at the car. We stop outside a house right next to the church. A woman is waiting at the front door. She walks towards the car.

'This is Miss Chambers,' says the social worker.

Her hand is on my back. Miss Chambers is younger than my ma but not as pretty. Her hair is light brown and swept back from her face. There is no colour on her skin except for the shadows under her small eyes. Her nose is long and comes to a point. Her teeth are yellow.

We step into the hallway of the house. It smells of polish and cabbage and fish. Morag stands against the wall. I stand beside her. The two women talk above us. I want to go home.

The social worker shakes Miss Chambers' hand then kneels down in front of us.

'Be good,' she says, tucking my hair behind my ear. 'I'll tell your mummy how brave you've both been.'

She turns to wave at the door and then she's gone. Miss Chambers locks the door behind her. I turn to face the wall. It feels cold against my head. The woman tries to get me to turn around.

'You can call me Auntie Vera,' she says. My neck is hot. The collar of my coat is sticking to it. I want Morag to do something.

'Your mum will visit soon,' she says, kneeling behind me. She grips my shoulders and pulls me around to face her. I lose my balance.

'Babies who cry don't get cake,' she says, and starts undoing the buttons on my coat. I look at Morag. She's wiping her eyes with her sleeve. Her nose is red and shiny. I don't want this woman to take my coat off. I don't want to stay.

'We'll get this off and hung up, then you can go through to the dining room and have some tea.'

I bend my arms. The coat gets stuck at my elbows. If she can't get it off then it means I can't stay. Vera pulls one arm straight and tugs hard at the sleeve. Her nails dig into my arm. I look at her to see if she knows what she's just done. Vera carries on taking my coat off. She hangs it over the rail on the stairs. I rub at my arm.

'Whit ur you cunts starin at?' says Morag to two girls standing in a doorway off the hall. One of them laughs and puts her hand to her mouth. The other keeps staring.

'We'll have no bad language out of you, young lady,' says Vera. 'You're not in Glasgow now.' She turns to the others. 'And as for the rest of you, it's about time you sat up at the table.'

They walk past us slowly. In the dining room there are three long tables. Five people are sitting round the middle one, four sit at the table nearest the hatch and three are sitting at the table opposite. We sit at the table with three.

There's a telly and some chairs at the bottom end of the room. The wall in front of me has photographs of children in school uniforms. I can smell chips. Everyone lowers their heads. *For what we are about to receive may the Lord make us truly thankful.*

The boy at the end of our table gets up and stands at the square-shaped hole in the wall. We are given the first two plates, fish fingers, chips and peas. I don't like peas.

A plate of buttered bread, cut into triangles, sits near the centre of the table. Morag makes a piece with her chips and I do the same. Five slices of sponge cake, with jam and coconut on the top, are sitting on a plate next to the bread. They look nice.

A younger woman with short curly hair puts a jug of milk and a bowl of sugar in the middle of our table. I've never seen anyone with hair as long as that. She comes back a few seconds later with a big metal teapot. The others on the table turn their cups the right way up and move to the side to let her pour. She's got hairy arms.

Morag's nearly finished. She's got one fish finger and a few chips left on her plate. The boy at the end finishes first. He takes the biggest slice of cake. Morag gets the next biggest. I can't eat the peas. I squash them with my fork but it just makes it look like there's more on the plate. We're the last two at the table.

'What's wrong with the peas?' asks Vera.

'I don't like them,' I say, and put my fork down. She stacks the rest of the dishes neatly and scrapes my peas onto the top plate.

'Well you'll have to get to like them, madam,' she says, pushing the last piece of cake towards me. She holds the plates against her and heads for the hatch. Morag licks her finger and dabs it in the crumbs of sponge and coconut.

Straight after tea, Vera takes us up to a shop where they give you new clothes; it's called the Drapery. You don't pay for them; they just give them to you. I get a school uniform, pants, shoes, vests, dresses, jumpers, socks, a cardigan, slippers, a dressing gown, pyjamas and a duffle coat. Morag won't try anything on, even when Vera pokes her in the chest. Morag pushes her hand away and tells her to fuck off. Vera slaps her hard but Morag doesn't cry.

Vera better watch herself. My ma could batter her easy. If Morag tells her about the slap then Vera's a dead woman. My ma's a good fighter. She gave the woman up the stairs from us a black eye because she'd been *askin for it*. My ma's not scared of anybody, not even my da and he's a good fighter.

14

My new school uniform is folded in a pile on the chair beside my bed. It looks like a present. The tie sits on the top. It's a snake, waiting for music. Morag's bed is next to mine. She's sitting up with her arms folded.

I like my bed. The sheets feel thick and soft. I like the smell of shampoo in my hair and the stiffness of my pyjamas. The pillow is smooth and heavy. I can taste the pink toothpaste in my mouth.

'Ugly cunt,' says Morag, kicking at her blankets. 'Fuckin bed at seven o'clock.'

She folds her arms tighter into herself. I don't mind getting sent to bed. The other kids are too big. They push past you and bang you out of their way. They laugh when somebody gets hit, or cries, or gets told off by Vera.

'Ah told er we stay up till eleven or twelve an aw she says is *You're not at home now, young lady.*'

Morag puts on a posh voice when she speaks like Vera and tilts her head back so that her nose sticks up. 'Ah wish tae fuck ah wis back hame,' she says, turning over onto her side.

'So do ah,' I say, but I really like this bed.

15

The new shirt feels nice, even when the buttons won't go in the holes. Morag keeps pulling at the waistband on her grey school skirt.

'Itches like fuck.'

The other two girls in the room have already gone downstairs. Mary's the eldest. She sleeps in the corner bed. Her hair's dead long. She came to bed after us and Morag was asking her loads of questions. She's from Maryhill and her two brothers sleep in the smaller boys' room. I wanted to ask her if she was called Mary because of where she came from but Morag was talking to her for ages.

'Canny breathe in this fuckin gear.' Morag pulls at the shirt collar and sticks her chin right out. Her face is getting red. I stand in front of the big wooden dressing table with the three mirrors. I look nice. The tie doesn't look right but neither does Morag's.

'BREAKFAST!' Vera shouts from the bottom of the stairs.

We sit in the same seats as last night. Nobody speaks. I don't know if it's because they're not allowed to or because they can't be bothered. Vera says, *For what we are . . .* and everybody joins in. Their heads are all down and some of them have their hands together. I look at Morag. She's trying not to laugh. When it's finished they take the small plates off the tops of their bowls and start putting milk on the cornflakes. The young woman with the short curly hair comes round with the teapot. You can feel the heat from it when she leans through the seats to get to the cup.

They call her Sarah, she doesn't sleep here. She left about eight o'clock last night. Slices of toast are stacked high on a plate in the middle of the table. You can eat as much as you like.

'Remember, Shona, to give that note to the teacher. Be back here before eleven, Auntie Sarah will go with you to the dentist.'

Shona nods at Vera. She's the other girl in our room. She said she's waiting to get put into Cottage 5, where her big brother is. Her dad is French and he works in a big hotel and her granny might let them go and live with her. I told her my ma's getting a new house and when she's better, we're going back to Glasgow. She asked what was up with my ma and Morag told her she fell down the stairs. We don't have stairs in our house. Morag tried asking her some more questions but she said, 'You'd better get to sleep or you'll get in trouble.'

Morag said, 'Trouble ma arse . . . that cunt comes near me an she'll get it.'

They start to get up from the table. Some clear the plates away, some tuck the chairs back under the table and some go into the kitchen. Vera shouts 'TEETH!' to the ones that are heading out of the door. Sarah takes a cloth to the middle table. Morag is still sitting opposite me. She has crumbs at the side of her mouth. Vera points to the door.

'Follow the others down to the bathroom and give your faces a quick wash and clean your teeth. Come back when you're finished to let me have a look at you.'

I follow Morag through the playroom and out the bottom door, past the wall with the shoes, down some steps that take you into the bathroom. Just above my head is a shelf with holes cut out to let the mugs with the toothbrushes sit in. A long line of cloths hangs on hooks. There is a name above each hook. Mine is the tenth. My cloth is yellow and my toothbrush is blue. The tin of toothpaste is small and the lid is hard to get off. Morag opens it for me. We watch the three boys at the basins. They wet the brush, rub it into the powder and put it in their mouths. Pink froth drips onto their chins. The biggest boy starts flicking his brush at the boy next to him. He's got gingery blond hair and loads of freckles. He doesn't look like he's got any eyelashes.

'Don't, Malkey, she'll go mad if it's aw er ma jumper.' Malkey laughs and spits whatever's left in his mouth straight into the boy's face and waits to see what he will do. Malkey's taller than the other two and his back is wider. His hands are almost as big as my da's. The boy with toothpaste all over his face doesn't say anything. I look at Morag but she's staring at Malkey.

The boy picks up his cloth and wipes at his face and clothes. He puts everything back in his mug and leaves the bathroom. I look at Morag again. She tilts her head in the direction of the sink. I follow her. Malkey rinses his mouth. It sprays over the edges of the sink.

'Put ma stuff away, an clean up the rest ay the mess,' he says, as he heads towards the door. The other boy nods at him and carries on brushing his teeth. Malkey punches five mugs straight out of their holes. Tins, brushes and plastic mugs bounce across the floor.

'Prick,' says the boy, under his breath.

16

Vera walks really fast. When she passes other grown-ups she says, 'Good morning ... lovely day,' but she doesn't stop. Her hair doesn't bounce at the back like my ma's. It doesn't move at all.

'We're in the very fortunate position of having our own school within the grounds at McGregor's; Nursery, Primary and Secondary.' Vera isn't talking to us, she's talking to herself as she walks. 'All five hundred children in our care attend. Much easier than bussing children out to local schools.'

We follow her down a road that leads to a big gate and a massive stone archway. The road is darker because of all the trees on either side. I can hear birds but I can't see them. They sound nice. Vera slows down to let us catch up.

We walk past the rows of parked cars at the front of the building. Vera holds one of the big double doors open for us. We have to go under her arm to get inside. There are two doors, one on either side. Vera pushes us towards the one on the left. A tall woman, wearing bright-red lipstick, gets up from behind a desk. Vera starts talking to her and showing her the papers she gets out of her bag. The woman behind the desk starts writing things down.

'I'll take them along, Miss Chambers, introduce them to their new teachers.'

Vera walks to the door. 'Best behaviour, mind ... I don't want any bad reports from your teachers.' I nod. Morag doesn't look up.

The woman with the red lipstick takes us to the other end of the school. The corridors are quiet and smell of warm dust. We walk on shiny wooden floors and climb stairs made of smooth stone. Morag's not happy. She's walking slowly and she won't take her hands out of her pockets. The woman with the red lipstick doesn't notice. We stop outside a classroom right at the end of the corridor. Morag is told to wait outside. The woman walks me to the front of the class. All the children are sitting on a piece of red carpet in front of the desks with their legs crossed.

'Good morning, Miss Lockie ... we have a new addition to your class today. This is Ailsa ...'

The woman with the red lipstick has her hands on my shoulders.

'Say hello, Ailsa ... this is your teacher, Miss Lockie.'

Miss Lockie has got the biggest diddies I've ever seen. Massive, pointy diddies. I look at Morag who's watching through the glass on the door. She's got both hands over her mouth and I can tell she's really laughing. I start giggling.

'I think Ailsa's a bit shy, Miss Lockie.'

I turn away from Morag and say hello to the teacher. The woman with the red lipstick leaves the classroom.

'Marjorie, can you take Ailsa down to the cloakroom and show her where to hang her coat?' A girl with big legs and curly hair uncrosses her legs and stands up. She's wearing the same kind of navy-blue knickers as me. I follow her down to the cloakroom and put my duffle coat on top of hers. She has a sticker beside her peg, a shiny red umbrella. When we get back to the classroom, Miss Lockie is sitting on a chair at the front.

'Today we are going to learn a song about a very famous

river in Scotland. This river travels all the way from the Leadhills down to the sea. Does anyone know the name of this river?'

17

Morag's waiting at the school gate. Her duffle coat is tied around her waist. I show her the gold star on my jumper.

'Whit did ye get that fur?'

'Miss Lockie says ah wis good at puttin ma hand up an foldin ma arms when we hud tae be quiet.'

Morag tightens the knot round her waist. 'Your teacher's got massive diddies, in't she? Did ye see the size ay them? Fucksake ... like big pointy mountains.'

I'd forgotten about Miss Lockie's diddies. I'd stopped noticing them after a while.

'She sang a song aboot the River Clyde, Morag, an ah told er, oor hoose is right next tae the River Clyde an sometimes ye kin see rats swimmin in the water but she said there wis no rats in the song we were gonnay learn about the River Clyde.'

Morag pulls her jumper into two points at the front, as far as they'll go, and starts wiggling at me.

'Watch oot,' she shouts, 'ma diddies'll get ye.'

I look around to see if anyone's watching.

'She gave me a tin, Morag, wi words inside, an if ah learn them all by the morra, she said I might get another star.'

Morag's not listening. 'Make way fur the massive diddies,' she shouts, 'they'll squash ye tae death.'

Some of the other kids are looking at her and laughing. She giggles and covers her mouth with one hand, which means she's only got one diddy. This makes them laugh even more.

I press the gold star to my chest and think about where I can keep it so that I can show it to my ma when she comes to get us.

18

Everybody has to do a job. My job this week is tidying the shed. The older kids have to do the harder jobs but the younger ones get it easier. Tidying the shed means you have to make sure all the duffle coats are hanging up, the wellingtons are off the floor and on the rack, the bikes are stacked up neatly against the wall and there are no potato peelings left under the sink. Sometimes you have to brush the shed floor with the hard brush you use to sweep the yard but only if Vera tells you to, otherwise you leave the floor for the next person.

The hardest jobs are the ones that are done for everybody. If you're on washing dishes for the week then it's washing breakfast, dinner and tea dishes for fourteen people. Same if you're on drying dishes, although there's usually two for drying. If you're on potatoes, it's peeling enough to fill a massive pot for dinner every day. Shoes are done every night except Friday so that you always have clean shoes for school and church.

The milkcan seems like an easy job but it isn't. The men from the local farm deliver it early in the morning. If you're on the milkcan you have to carry the four gallons from the end of the path, into the cottage and through to the pantry in the kitchen. You then have to place two of the big metal jugs on the floor, tip the milkcan forward getting the position just right and fill them up. The metal jugs are then put in the fridge and you have to make sure they're topped up throughout the day. At night you have to clean out the milkcan with hot soapy water and rinse it a few times before carrying it out to the end of the path for the milkmen in the morning. The can smells funny by the end of the day and even though you use soapy water, you can still smell it on your fingers.

The dining-room job is probably the best. Nobody stands over you when you clear the tables, wash the tables, sweep the floor and set the tables for the next meal. All the adults are usually in the kitchen, making sure the dishes are being done properly.

The easy jobs are the shed, sweeping the yard, dusting the hall and polishing the playroom floor. When Vera's in a good mood, she lets you tie the cloths to your feet and slide up and down the playroom floor. Once your jobs are done you're free to go out and play.

19

'Ah'm gonnay walk tae the top ay the hill, Morag, see if the bus is comin.'

Morag is sitting on the wall. 'It'll be here in a minute, just wait.'

I don't want to wait; it's taking too long. I want to see what's on the other side of the hill.

'We kin race it back doon an see who's the winner.'

Morag jumps off the wall. 'C'mon then.'

Saturdays are good. You get visitors and pocket money and the dinner's good as well. Mary says it's always pie and chips, bridie and chips or sausage roll and chips. The first week it was sausage roll and chips, last week it was pie and chips, that was lovely, and today it was sausage rolls again.

'Any sweeties left?'

I make out like I'm feeling around in my pockets while I think about whether to tell her about my last caramel. If I don't tell her I won't be able to eat it until she's gone and she's come up the hill with me even though she couldn't be bothered.

'Just a caramel, ye kin huv a bit if ye want.' I unwrap it and put my thumb up to the bit where she can bite. Her head shakes from side to side until her teeth have bitten through. I have the rest.

You have to line up outside Vera's sitting room for the pocket money. She asks you if your job is done and when you say yes she gets out an envelope with your name on from a big tin and gives you two bob. The older ones get more, the younger ones get less. They opened a tuck shop at the back of the store. It only stays open for an hour and you have to squeeze your way to the front of the queue. I got a bar of Highland toffee, two lollipops and some caramels, Morag got two sherbets, chocolate and a gobstopper.

'Whit dinner d'ye like best, Morag? Ah like the pie an chips.'

While Morag's thinking about it I remember the fish and chips on a Thursday, battered or breadcrumbs.

'Mince an doughballs, but no the cabbage,' says Morag at last.

I think about the fish and chips and the pie. The pie still wins. 'D'ye think they'll come the day, Morag?'

Morag picks up a stone and throws it at a cow in the field. It flicks its tail and carries on eating. She buttons up her duffle coat. 'If my ma's better, they'll come doon.'

The hill isn't as high as it looks. On the other side there are more fields and cows. The road bends at the bottom of the hill. Dark-green trees hide it. My ears are starting to get cold. Morag throws stones at the new cows but they're too far away.

I can hear the bus but I can't see it. The noise is getting louder. I keep my eyes on the trees for the first sign of it. Morag pushes the hair back from her face.

'It's comin, c'mon.'

'Wait till we see it first.' It sounds like the bus but it could be a lorry or a tractor.

'There, under the trees.' Morag points to where I'm looking. It's small, like a white painted box. Morag starts running. It's going to be easy to beat it running downhill. I pull at Morag's coat. She laughs and shakes me off. My legs move without me really trying. We're halfway down the hill when the bus gets to the top of it. I run my hardest.

I've nearly caught up with Morag. She turns to see where the bus is. I pull at her coat and keep hold.

'Fuck off, Puddin, yer slowin me doon,' she laughs.

I let go. She's going too fast, I can't keep up. The bus passes me. Morag touches the bus shelter just before the bus pulls in. It's full. We stand in front of the doors while the people get off.

'Good wee runner, in't ye, hen?' shouts the driver. Morag doesn't answer him.

'Next time ah'll beat ye.'

Morag moves away from the bus and stands against the wall. I'm still trying to catch my breath. An old woman with grey hair is the last person to get off the bus. They're not there.

I look at Morag. She's twisting the toggles on her duffle coat. I sit on the ground beside her and listen to the bus until I can't hear it anymore.

'Let's climb on top ay the bus shelter an sit there fur a wee while.' Morag pulls herself up onto the wall.

'Yer no allowed, Morag. Vera'll go mad if she finds oot.'

'Fuck er, she's no here. It's just fur a wee while, see whit it's like.'

There's no way I'm going up on the bus shelter. When Vera goes mad she goes *really* mad, like with Maisie McCreedy's cot. I had to change the wet sheets and put on clean ones but I forgot the rubber mat that's supposed to go on first. Vera came into the bedroom and started screaming. She banged my head off the bars on the cot and stuck the rubber mat in my face. *Are you stupid? Are you altogether thick?* She pushed it into my face until I was up against the wall. The smell was catching on my throat. When I started crying she punched me on the side of the head. *Shut up . . . shut up . . .* She said it quietly, through her teeth. I knew the crying was making her worse but I didn't know how to stop. She pulled my hand away from my head and punched it again in the same place. I kept my lips and teeth tight together to keep the sounds in but my chest kept making noises. It was me that was making her angry. I stopped looking at her and looked at the floor instead. *Strip it back down ... useless imbecile ... do it properly or woe betide you ...* There's no way I'm going up on the bus shelter.

The sun's gone. Morag's legs dangle from the top of the shelter. 'Ye kin see inty the main office fae here, the desk an the cupboards.'

I'm not bothered about seeing into the main office. The main office is stupid. I twist the toggles on my duffle coat as tight as I can then I let them go because I think it might be sore for the little bit of rope that goes through the toggle. What if the rope is screaming really loud and I can't hear it? What if the other bits of rope on the other toggles are its family and can see him twisting and scream-ing and can't save him? I pat the toggle and straighten it out gently.

Two shapes come over the top of the hill. My whole body feels like it's watching. There's something about the way the shapes move. I get up from the ground and start to run. The nearer I get the surer I am.

My da kneels down and opens his arms. 'C'mon, Puddin, c'mon, hen.'

I can hear Morag's feet behind me. His coat smells of our house in Wallace Street. My ma is cuddling into me.

'Look at them, Gina, they're brand new – fuckin magic.'

My ma's hands touch my face and hair. They keep grab-bing us and squeezing hard. My ma lifts me up. Her hair smells like marshmallows. My da's got a bag with two bottles of Irn-Bru and millions of sweeties in it. Morag says she'll carry the bag. My ma wipes her eyes with the back of her hand. She cannot stop smiling. My ma and da are movie stars. Morag's telling my da how she beat the bus and climbed on top of the bus shelter. My ma holds my hand, her thumb keeps moving over my skin. She squeezes it as we walk through the main gates.

Morag takes them round the long way and I'm glad. Everybody can see our visitors and how beautiful they are.

'That's the Drapery, Ma, they gie ye new claes an everythin.'

My ma twists her head to see it. I show her my new jumper under my duffle coat. She smiles. 'Smart duds, hen, ye look lovely.'

Morag points to her left. 'That's the church, Da, they make ye go twice on a Sunday. It's borin as fuck an the minister goes on fur ages an ages.'

My da laughs and looks at my ma. 'Church, eh? Whit next?'

My ma starts crying. 'It looks lovely, disn't it, Frankie? The flowers an the grass an that.' She gets a hankie out of her pocket.

'Plenty a space fur ye tae run aroon, lassies, eh?' He puts his arm round my ma's shoulders. 'They're brand new, Gina, look at them.'

I don't want my ma to cry. 'Ye get big dinners, Ma, pie an chips an mince an doughballs.'

My da throws his head back and laughs really loud. 'You tell er, Puddin, fresh air fortnight, eh?'

My ma stops crying by the time we get to the cottage. Vera opens the door.

'Afternoon,' says my da.

Vera holds the door open until we're all in the hallway.

'Nice to see you, Mr and Mrs Dunn. We didn't get any word about a visit this weekend.'

My ma and da look at each other.

'Are ye supposed tae get permission or somethin?' My da looks at Vera.

'No, no, Mr Dunn, not at all, it's just we usually hear from the social worker or someone in the family to say there'll be a visit.' Vera looks at her watch. Morag pulls my da towards the playroom. Vera's telly is blaring in her sitting room.

'We missed the bus,' says my ma. 'We've walked the couple a miles fae the village up the road.'

'Not to worry,' says Vera, 'we'll get the kettle on and make some tea.' My ma and da look at each other again. Vera heads towards the kitchen.

'Whit's yer name, hen?' says my da holding out his hand.

'Miss Chambers,' says Vera coming back from the kitchen. She shakes my da's hand.

'Pleased tae meet ye, hen – the wains look well.'

Vera folds her arms across her chest. 'Well, Mr Dunn, Ailsa's bed-wetting is a real problem. We're thinking of letting the doctor have a look at her.' My face and neck get really hot. My ma squeezes my hand.

'It's probably aw the upset,' says my ma. 'She wis gettin really good fur a dry bed at hame.'

Vera doesn't say anything. Morag pulls at my da's arm again.

'And Morag's been taken to task on more than one occasion for her colourful language, Mr Dunn, but apart from that they've settled in well enough.'

Vera's trying to spoil it. She's trying to get us into trouble with my ma and da.

'C'mon, Da.' Morag pulls his coat sleeve towards the playroom door.

'We'll huv a wee word, Miss Chambers.' My da follows Morag into the playroom. We sit at the window, around the table.

'Cheeky cunt,' says my ma. 'Whit the fuck dis she expect?'

My da puts the bag on the table. Morag dives in. 'Share it oot equally, there's two ay everythin.'

Morag makes two piles. My ma lights a fag.

'Take yer coat aff, Gina, ye'll no get the benefit.' My da pulls me up onto his knee. 'Don't worry aboot the bed-wettin, Puddin, ye'll grow ooty it. Aw wains huv wee accidents.'

Vera comes in with the tray. My da puts me down and gets up to give her a hand.

'Thanks very much, hen – just whit the doctor ordered.' My da puts the tray on the table.

Vera opens the window above my ma's head. 'Ailsa, get your mother an ashtray from the cupboard under the sink.' My ma's still got her coat on.

'We'll take them oot fur a wee walk, hen, efter the tea, get oot fae under yer feet.'

'Not at all, Mr Dunn, you're more than welcome.' Vera shuts the door quietly behind her.

Morag sticks her two fingers up at the door.

My ma smiles, puts her fag in the ashtray and takes her coat off. 'Stuck-up cunt.'

20

Vera likes Sundays the best. I think it's because she gets dressed up and puts on a bit of lipstick. She really likes those suits where the coat matches the dress and her bag is the same colour as her shoes. She sometimes wears the gloves but mostly she just carries them.

We get into line about quarter to eleven along the wall beside the front door. Vera pats down hair, straightens collars and points to rolled-down socks.

'You'll be on your best behaviour, mind. If I so much as hear a peep out of any of you, woe betide you.' She gives you the look and you know she's deadly serious.

Vera leads the walk to the church. We follow the paths in a neat line. She smiles at all the other adults, 'Good morning, beautiful day, isn't it?'

It should really only take two minutes to get to the church as our cottage is right next to it but Vera likes to walk round to the top door and take us from the back of the church right down to the front.

Every cottage has its own pews. Ours are right at the front on the left-hand side. The pews are divided into three sections; a wide centre section with long pews and shorter pews on the right- and left-hand sides.

Vera keeps the naughtiest children on either side of her. The ones who might misbehave are either in front of her or near enough to her so that she can poke at them or give them a good nip.

You're not allowed to flick through the pages of the hymn book or the Bible, you're not allowed to pick at any scabs you might have. You're not allowed to talk or listen to anyone else other than the minister and you're not allowed to play games with your feet with the people on either side of you.

When the minister talks I mostly think about what my ma and da might be doing in Glasgow and if Mrs Fisher still lives up the stairs. I think about Doanal and Big Isa and why they don't come down to visit. Sometimes I count the bits of dandruff on Malkey's shoulders or the flowers in the vases at the front of the church. The singing is quite good in the church and Vera knows most of the tunes, she just squeaks a bit when it comes to the high notes.

When the service is over, people leave the church one row at a time, starting from the back. Vera always stops to chat to the other adults. She doesn't mind you walking back to the cottage on your own as long as she doesn't catch you running.

The first thing she does when she gets back from the church is change out of her good clothes. Sarah has already started dishing up the dinner. Vera hands out the last few plates then sits down to eat her dinner.

'We'll be going for a nice walk after dinner so don't stray too far.'

The nice walk lasts for five miles; two miles into Bridge of Weir, a mile up the hill to the posh houses and two miles back to the Homes. Vera especially likes it if she gets the chance to say good afternoon to the people who live in the posh houses or chat to them about how *good brisk walks never did them any harm*.

Sarah doesn't go to the evening service. She baths the younger ones and makes sure they're all in bed by the time Vera comes back. The rest of us take turns to go for our bath. There's never anything good on the telly on a Sunday night so there's not much fighting about who goes in and when. Vera shouts the names for bedtime from her sitting room on the hour and half-hour. Everyone is in bed sharp for school the next day.

21

I was only asking Mary if it was the man with the glasses who killed the woman in the film.

'You've been warned about this umpteen times, young lady, I'm sick to the back teeth of telling you to be quiet at bedtime.'

I always end up crying when Vera takes me to the shed. I think it's the way she bursts into the bedroom and the way her nails dig into the side of my neck when she drags me down the stairs.

'Too late for tears now, madam, you should have thought about that before opening your big mouth. A couple of hours on your own will soon sort you out.'

When Vera shouts at Morag, she answers her back. *Get yer paws aff. Ah know where the shed is.* Then every time Vera says something after that Morag'll say, *So what. Big fuckin deal.* Vera's usually in her nightie when she lets Morag out of the shed.

I can hear the telly in the dining room. Malkey and Derek must still be up. She'll probably send me to bed when they go up.

Vera has a tight grip as she pushes me through the bottom playroom door and out past the shoe rack where the bathroom and toilet are. She unlocks the door that leads to the shed and pushes me in. 'We'll see how much of a chatterbox you are after a spell in here, young lady.'

She locks the door and slams the playroom door shut as she heads back to her sitting room. It's pitch black. That's when I feel at the wall for the duffle coats hanging on the rack. I take one to wrap round my feet and the other to put on properly. Morag told me about the duffle coats.

The shed has a tin roof and a concrete floor. The door leading from the back of the cottage into the shed has a step. That's where you're supposed to sit until Vera comes to let you out. It has one of those brown jaggy mats for wiping your feet on before you go into the cottage.

There is a brick wall along the left-hand side, which has two rows of metal hooks for the duffle coats. The hooks stop halfway along the wall because of the door for the shed toilet. The wall facing has a low wooden shelf that holds the wellington rack. The wellingtons are turned upside down and individually placed over a short wooden pole so that they don't get lost or piled up in a heap.

The right-hand wall is brick on the bottom and windows on the top. There are eight panes of glass altogether. The wooden back door is at the bottom end of this wall. The wall with the step has the old sink to the right of it, where the potatoes get peeled, and a big brown sack of potatoes is kept underneath.

I didn't hear her on the stairs. She takes her Scholls off at the bottom and sneaks up really quietly. Sometimes you hear a creak and everyone stops whispering and listens really hard for ages. She must be like a statue until the whispering starts again.

I think Vera either grabs the person who was last to speak or the person she's heard speaking the most as she's been coming up the stairs. Either way, nobody speaks after Vera's been in.

I mostly think about my ma and da in the shed and what they'd do to Vera if they ever found out what she was really like. I imagine her getting dragged by the hair across the playroom floor by my ma and her screaming she's sorry and she didn't mean it, then my da picks us up and carries us out to McAllister's car and we drive back to Glasgow.

22

There's a big shadow at the side of the bed. The hands pulling on my pyjamas are heavy. At first I think it's Auntie Vera checking to see if I'm dry but the shadow's got short hair.

'Who's that?' I sit up, and the hands come out from under the blankets.

Malkey Donnelly gets up off his knees and starts straightening the covers. 'It's awright,' he whispers. 'Go tae sleep, ah'm just tuckin ye in.' He holds the front of his pyjamas and tiptoes out of the room.

Everybody else is asleep. Morag turns over. Her mouth is open. The landing creaks then a few seconds later the toilet flushes.

'Morag.' The whisper sounds really loud. 'Morag.' I pull up my pyjamas and lie on my belly. I listen for noises on the stairs.

23

I don't really like Marjorie Curry. She's fat and sits with her legs open and you can see right up her skirt. Even when you tell her to shut them, they fall open again after a couple of minutes. She's got two big raw patches at the tops of her legs on the inside and she smells funny, like the empty milkcan. She sometimes calls for me to go out and play but I don't like going out with her. She's not as good a fighter as Morag. When you go out with Morag, nobody starts on you; nobody takes your stuff off you. If you've got big brothers and sisters people leave you alone. I'm swapping my skipping ropes for her Cindy but we have to go to her piano lesson first.

The music room is at the very top of the main hall, where they sometimes show films on a Saturday morning. I didn't know there were rooms this high up in the building. The staircase gets narrower and darker. I think of Rapunzel.

'Don't laugh, Ailsa, if ah make a mistake, ah huvny practised very much.'

Marjorie's bum wobbles under her skirt. It looks heavy. She's holding her piano book in one hand and my skipping ropes in the other. I can hear a piano playing. We're almost there.

Marjorie knocks on the door and the music stops. Her teacher stands up as we enter the room. He smiles.

'Is it awright if ma pal waits fur me, Mr Shaugnessy?' asks Marjorie, moving towards the piano. I follow her into the room.

'Of course she can,' he says, still smiling.

Mr Shaugnessy is small and almost bald. His nose is long and straight. I find a seat against the back wall while Marjorie drags the piano stool nearer to the piano and finds the right page in her book. Mr Shaugnessy sits in a chair beside her. He leans over her to stop the page turning back on itself and slides a little pin upwards to keep it in place. His hands don't touch her.

Marjorie plays up and down the piano with her right hand, then up and down the piano with her left. I want to touch the instruments that are lying around but it feels like you have to be quiet and be good in this room. The music on her page looks like black caterpillars.

'C major, contrary motion . . .' Marjorie's fingers move again.

'E flat major, two octaves . . .'

'G minor arpeggio, left hand, four octaves . . .'

I like the word *arpeggio*.

'Excellent, Marjorie, some of the fingering is tricky and you remembered about the elbows.' He pats her on the back. His hands don't stay on her.

Marjorie plays a proper tune next, two hands together, slowly. There are more new words: *crescendo*, *tempo*, *mezzo forte*. When she gets to the end he plays it for her properly. The notes sound like coloured ribbons. Marjorie picks at the scab on her knee. When he finishes I nearly clap.

'The dynamics are very important, Marjorie.'

Marjorie nods her head quickly and stands to the side of the piano. I think she is finished but Mr Shaugnessy plays a short tune and she has to clap the rhythm of it back to him. She can't do it. She gets some of it right but never all of it. I tap them quietly on the side of my chair. They're easy, like the rhythms in words:

kettle-kettle-bang-bang-slippery-bang-kettle-bang. I tap louder so that he will hear.

'Can you do these?' he asks. I nod. He plays a different tune, twice, and then turns to me. I clap it back: *kettle-bang-slippery-bang*. The next one's harder: *tapioca-tapioca-slippery-kettle-bang*. His eyes go big. He's nodding his head and smiling.

'One more?'

I listen hard while he plays the tune through twice. *Humpty-Dumpty-slippery-kettle-Humpty-Dumpty-bang*.

'What an excellent ear you've got, I'm very impressed.' He talks through his smile.

'You should think about learning an instrument,' he says, 'with an ear like that.'

Marjorie is standing beside the door. She is holding her books and skipping ropes. I don't want to go. I want to stay in this room and clap rhythms with Mr Shaugnessy.

'Cheerio,' shouts Marjorie. I can hear her feet on the stairs. Mr Shaugnessy starts looking for something on top of the piano.

'Kin ah learn the piano, Mr Shaugnessy?'

He stops what he is doing and looks straight at me. 'You most certainly can, young lady, but it'll have to be after the summer holidays now.'

I nod at him and smile.

'You come back and see me in September,' he says, 'and we'll get you started straight away.'

I walk towards the door.

'God bless,' he says, and pats my head.

I feel like I've won a prize.

24

From the wall I can see the top of the hill where the bus comes down. I can see it turn round, drop off the passengers and go back up the hill. From where I sit you cannot miss a thing and I don't want to because today they'll come. I can feel it. My ma won't forget I'm eight on Tuesday and if she leaves it to next Saturday she'll have missed it. They'll come. I know they will.

Jeannie Bell and Carol Fletcher are marking out *beds* with a small chalky stone. It makes a nice scratching noise and they ask if we want to play. Morag goes over to watch them but I want to stay on the wall.

Mrs Forsythe, the minister's wife, stands inside the bus shelter to keep out of the sun. She's wearing a brown fur collar on a dark-green coat and a small black hat with a shiny peacock brooch. She wears that fur collar everywhere, at church, at the post office. She keeps dabbing at her face with her hankie. I'm glad she's in the bus shelter. Her breath really smells and if I look at her runny eyes too long it makes mine water. She's talking to one of the cottage aunties. Mrs Forsythe is telling her to eat more vegetables and wear less make-up.

The bus appears at the top of the hill, slowly rocking from side to side. It's too early for my ma and da but you never know. Mrs Forsythe is holding the hankie over her nose and mouth. The fumes catch my throat. As the bus turns round I can hear a man's voice from the inside. It sounds like he's shouting.

The doors hiss as they open and a tiny wee woman

steps off. She tightens her headscarf. Her face is beetroot.

'Shh, Archie . . . there's nae need fur language like that. It's a children's home fur God's sake . . . Huv some respect.'

The man sways as he steps off the bus.

'Ah'll use whitever language ah fuckin well like,' he says. He points to the people on the bus. 'An these snobby cunts urney gonnay stoap me.'

He points to the sky then he points at me. I smile. He winks. Swear words from grown-ups feel like a treat. I can almost smell them hanging in the air. They remind me of Shuggy and my da and Glasgow and Wallace Street.

'Ah don't give a fuck who's listenin.'

Archie seems to get bigger every time he opens his mouth and the woman gets smaller. She stops telling him to *shh* and walks quickly in front of him. Morag looks over and we laugh.

Mrs Forsythe *tut tut tuts* as she gets on the bus and mutters under her breath about *drunkards* and *louts* and *bringing back the birch*. The bus crawls away from the stop and disappears over the top of the hill.

'Will we follow them?' asks Morag, pulling herself up onto the wall beside me. 'They're a right showin up, let's see who they've come to visit?'

I know it would be funny and the drunk man seems really nice but I don't want to leave the bus stop, just in case.

'It won't be back fur ages,' says Morag.

'Ah'm jist gonnay wait here,' I tell her.

Morag follows behind Archie, staggering when he staggers and steadying herself when he does. Carol keeps asking him who they've come to visit.

*   *   *

Morag comes back a couple of hours later.

'Ye should've come,' she smiles. 'The wuman started greetin and sat doon on a bench. She said she widney go any further cos he wis a right showin up. Ah told her ah would go an get whoever it wis she'd come tae visit and she gied me a shillin.'

'Ye missed a big fight here,' I said, but it wasn't true. 'Two men started punchin each other an one of them had blood aw doon es coat an es eyes were aw puffed up an the bus driver split them up but the polis came an took them away.'

'Ah didny hear any polis car,' she says, finding a space beside me.

'It wis a van wi a big dog an it didny have any sirens.'

Morag is quiet.

'The wimin were screamin an everythin. It wis the worst fight ah've ever seen.'

'Well ah got a shillin an that's better than watchin a stupid fight.'

She jumps off the wall and picks up some stones and starts throwing them at the bus shelter. I hate it when she does stuff like this. Somebody'll come and shout at us both and I'm not even doing anything.

The bus comes over the top of the hill. It moves like an old roller coaster. This makes her stop. The passengers leave the bus. It's like an identity parade. I don't trust my eyes. Maybe I've missed them. I check the backs of staff and visitors for anything familiar. Mrs Forsythe reaches up and pokes my knee. I can see some leeks sticking out of the top of her carrier bag.

'You'll get a chill sitting there, young lady.'

I cannot speak. I have stones in my throat. Everything feels tight and ready to burst. I want to scream *Fuck off, ya old bag, with yer dirty breath and yer stupid brooch* but

I stare at my shoes and rub my thumbs, hard against the wall.

Morag starts. 'They're no comin, y'know. If they were comin they'd huv been here by noo. They huvney been fur weeks. Whit makes ye think they'll turn up the day?'

I shrug.

'It's a waste a bloody time, they're no fuckin comin.'

I jump down off the wall. The back of the bus disappears over the hill. I wish she'd stop.

'Let's go,' she says.

I shake my head.

'Ah'm goin.'

Morag throws the last of her stones at the shelter.

'Fuck off then,' I mutter under my breath.

The punch makes me lose my balance. It catches me on the side of the head.

'Don't tell me tae fuck off, ya cheeky fat cunt.'

Her face is close to mine. I rub my ear. The tears are a relief. The punch isn't that sore. I keep my head down. She thunders off, shouting about *stupid fuckin bus stops* and *useless, cuntin bastards*. I stay for a couple more trips just in case.

25

We're going to Turnberry for two weeks. It's beside the seaside. Mr Pitt, the millionaire, owns the houses at Turnberry and lets the Homes have them in the summer so that everybody gets a holiday. He's got a runway and a swimming pool and stables and horses. Me and Morag have to share a suitcase. Vera checks that we've got everything.

'Swimming costumes?'

I find my green costume with the pink fish on the front, right at the bottom of the case. Wilma, in the Drapery, was going to give me a brand new navy-blue one until I spotted the green one and asked for that. Morag pulls at the corner of some of her clothes to show that her costume is folded neatly under her shorts and T-shirts.

'Knickers?'

I lift my pile from the right-hand side of the suitcase and hold them out to let her see. Morag lifts hers from the left.

'Your case can go to the bottom of the stairs now and make sure you get straight to sleep because the bus'll be here sharp in the morning.'

Morag clicks the case shut while I push the lid down. She carries it down the stairs and puts it with the rest of the boxes, bags and cases. Ours is red with a brown handle. Morag doesn't go straight to bed. She leans against the window sill for a while and looks out of the window.

'D'ye think Turnberry's gonnay be good, Morag?'

'Ah think it'll be great, swimmin in the sea, strokin the horses . . .'

'Whit if Ma an Da come an wer no here?'

'Nay fear ay that, Puddin, they huvny been fur months.'

The holiday clothes are folded neatly on the chair beside my bed, pale-blue cords, pink T-shirt and white cardigan. Wilma in the Drapery likes me. She gets me to try the clothes on or holds them up against me and then lets me pick what I like best.

'Will the sea be like Loch Lomond, Morag?'

Morag thinks about it for a few seconds.

'Ah think the sea'll be bigger than Loch Lomond.'

26

Morag is first to spot the double-decker. Its wheels go right to the edge of the path. It moves really slowly through the trees like it might break them. Mary and Morag pull me up to the window sill so I can see. It stops outside our cottage where Malkey and Derek have stacked all the boxes and cases.

The driver lifts open a door at the side of the bus and starts loading them in. Sarah opens the playroom door.

'Anyone for the toilet goes now, we'll be leaving shortly and you won't get another chance.'

Morag and Mary don't move from the window sill.

'Keep me a seat if yer allowed on the bus.'

Morag nods. I follow Sarah out of the bottom door of the playroom, down the steps into the toilets. She lets me go first then stays to help the little ones get up onto the seat. The playroom is empty when I get back. I run out to the bus and climb the stairs. Morag has got a double front seat. She's sitting sideways on it with her legs across both seats. She moves her leg to let me sit down.

'This is the best seat, Morag. We kin see everythin fae up here.'

Morag leans forward and rests her arms against the metal rail that runs along the front window.

'That smoke fae oot the back ay the bus is makin me feel sick awready.'

'Once it gets goin ye kin stick yer heid up tae that wee windy there an get some fresh air.'

Vera gets to the top of the stairs and starts counting

heads. She turns and shouts 'OK' to the driver. She manages to get to the bottom deck before the bus starts to move. Morag puts her head near the small, open window above her. I duck when the branches of the trees slam against the top of the bus.

'Daft cunt,' Morag laughs.

The bus rolls from side to side and you have to keep your feet apart and hold onto the metal rail so you don't slip off your seat. It's great being right at the front; you can see the tops of people's heads and what the trees look like from up high.

The bus slows down to get through the main gates. The kids at the back start singing *The front ay the bus they canny sing* . . . We wave at people as we pass them. Morag gets more waves than me but she's got most of the side window, I've only got the front.

The suitcases and boxes are piled up outside the house that we're staying at. Vera is talking to a man who's showing her where everything is and pointing to the rooms upstairs. The kitchen is right in front of us. Mary nudges me.

'There's another room beside the kitchen that you canny see but it's got tables an chairs an that little shed is where the ice creams and ice lollies are kept. Mr Pitt fills it up tae the brim when a new cottage comes tae stay.'

The door to the shed has a padlock.

'Ah hope he disny forget the keys tae that.'

Mary nods. Morag is sitting on our suitcase. She had to lie across the two seats for most of the journey because she felt sick. She's starting to look a lot better.

'Whit are we waitin fur?'

Vera and the man come out of the main part of the house. He hands her the keys and starts loading some of the boxes into the kitchen. Vera stands in front of us.

'Girls' rooms upstairs, boys' rooms downstairs.'

Morag bombs it up the stairs. By the time I get up, there are only bottom bunks left. The one under Morag has a window. I put the suitcase beside that one.

Sarah comes round with pink nylon sheets and pillowcases.

'Once you've unpacked your case, take it down to the shed at the far end of the yard and make sure your clothes are folded neatly into the drawers and not just flung in. Soup and a sandwich in ten minutes.'

It's hard getting the corner bits of the sheet to go round the corners of the mattress. Morag helps. I lie on my finished bed to see what it feels like. You can see the field with the horses and the wood at the top of the hill. You cannot see the sea. Morag slams her drawer shut. I've got the third drawer down. It's easy to unpack; you just lift the pile of clothes out of the suitcase and put them straight into the drawer. Morag shuts the suitcase and holds it above her head as she leaves the bedroom.

'Ah want tae see whit this shed's like.'

The room next to the kitchen is a dining room. The floors are stone and they have stools around the tables instead of chairs. Sarah is ladling soup into plastic mugs. There are four tables here instead of the three we normally have. It looks like you can sit where you like.

Vera puts a plate of sandwiches on each table.

'Keep the same jobs you had for this week and we'll change them at the end of next week.'

Mine is the yard. It's dead easy. The tuna sandwiches are really nice.

'After your soup, get your costumes on underneath your clothes and we'll take a walk along to the beach.'

Morag nudges me to hurry up.

It seems daft putting your pants on, on top of your swimming costume. Morag doesn't. She wraps her pants

87

in her towel and pulls her trousers over her costume. I roll up my towel and follow her down the stairs. I like the stairs being on the outside of the building.

There is a line of people at the kitchen door. Vera has the pocket money tin in her lap. We join the queue.

'If you're good, you'll be getting pocket money every day.'

Morag turns to look at me. She makes a face that really means bloody hell. I smile back at her.

'But anyone who steps out of line while we're down here on holiday will be lucky to get pocket money after a month.'

Morag puts her two bob in her pocket. I hold onto mine for a while.

As we head out of the grounds, past the horses and the swimming pool, we see Mr Pitt the millionaire getting out of his shiny silver sports car. I don't know how he fits in it because he's really fat. I thought he'd look like James Bond. I thought he'd have gold rings on his fingers and smoke a cigar. He wobbles towards Vera moving from side to side like Charlie Chaplin.

'Good morning. How're you finding the accommodation?'

Vera smiles the same smile she gives to all the adults. 'Perfect, Mr Pitt, absolutely perfect, it's so lovely to meet you.'

'And Mr Docherty, he showed you where everything was?'

'Mr Docherty was extremely helpful, thank you.'

Mr Pitt the millionaire has a double chin and a sweaty face.

'Well enjoy your holiday and don't hesitate to call on Docherty's services should you need them.'

'Thank you, Mr Pitt, we certainly will.'

Mr Pitt wobbles off to the field to have a look at his horses. Vera looks at the rest of us to give him a wave and say goodbye.

'Bye . . . Bye . . .'

The walk to the beach takes ages and has to be done in single file because the road doesn't have any pavements. Vera leads the way; Sarah stays at the back, carrying the bag with the plastic beakers and the bottles of diluted orange juice.

The village is called Maidens and isn't very big. It has a paper shop, a VG store and a shop that sells nails and hammers. The shops are all on the same side. You cross the main road, walk over some grass and you're on the beach. The VG store has two big baskets at the entrance. One is full of beach balls; the other is full of bucket-and-spade sets. Vera buys a bright orange beach ball and three sets of buckets and spades. We're allowed to spend our pocket money at the paper shop. The man stays behind the till. The woman comes out to watch us while we're in the shop. Morag gets two bars of Highland toffee and some crisps. I get Opal Fruits and one bar of Highland toffee.

Vera finds a good spot on the sand and spreads out the woollen rug. We have to leave our towels and shoes in a neat pile before we can go down to the water. Derek and Malkey have the ball. Vera gives me a yellow bucket with a blue starfish on the front and a matching blue spade.

'The buckets and spades are for everybody, I don't want any fighting, make sure you share.'

Vera rubs brown oil from a bottle onto her legs.

27

It's the last night and we're having a midnight campfire on the beach. Mary says it's great; you get hot dogs and juice and sit round the fire.

'Just lie on the top of your bed and we'll wake you up when it's time to go.'

I can't get to sleep. My clothes feel too tight and heavy. Our shoes are lined up near the door and our jackets are on the chair in the corner.

'Vera might fall asleep, Morag, an forget to wake up and then we'll no huv a campfire on the beach.'

'She's no goin tae sleep. Her an Sarah'll stay awake till it's time.'

'Whit if they're only kiddin about the campfire an they just want us tae sleep wi our claes on so we'll be ready fur the bus in the mornin?'

Mary turns to lie on her belly. 'She has a campfire every year. She always does it.'

I look out of the window at the horses eating grass in the field. Turnberry's great. Ice creams every day and pocket money and swimming.

It's dark when Sarah comes round the bedrooms. She switches on the light. 'Shoes and coats on, we'll be off in a minute.'

I've got a blanket to carry. Morag's got the bag with the plastic beakers. Everybody's got something. We walk in single file. It's pitch black except for the light from Vera's torch at the front of the line and Sarah's from the back.

'Keep well in to the side. I don't expect there to be any cars at this time of night but you never know.'

Sometimes you can hear funny noises from behind the hedges. I think it's the cows walking about. I have to take shorter steps because Morag keeps getting out of time when she stops to change the bag from one hand to the other and then Ryan McCreedy steps on my heels.

'Look at the stars, aren't they bright.'

Vera's walking with her head up to the sky. I hold the blanket in front of my face and look up. That way, if a branch from a bush is sticking out from the roadside it won't get me in the face.

I can see a few of the streetlights in the main part of the village. The houses are either in darkness or have a light on in their living rooms. We cross the main road while Vera stands in the middle hurrying everyone across. Everything is silent except for the noise from the sea.

'Have a look around for some small pieces of wood.'

Vera puts down her bag and starts scrumpling up old newspapers. I lay out my blanket and stay beside Sarah who looks for some sticks. Small handfuls of wood are brought to the fire. Vera puts the wood on top of the firelighters and paper. The wind blows out the first two matches. The third one lights the fire. Malkey and Derek come back with half a tree.

'It's far too big for the fire, Malcolm, use it to sit on.'

They position the log at the other side of the fire and sit down. Vera has a pile of wood at her side. The flames are only small but they make a lot of light. Everyone can see now. The others spread the rest of the blankets so that we all have something to sit on. We watch the fire get bigger. Vera's the only one allowed to go near it.

Sarah gets out the tins of hot dogs and the can opener. She places them straight onto the fire. The paper on the tin bubbles and blackens until you can't read the words anymore.

'Don't you need a pot, Auntie Sarah?'

Maisie McCreedy is sitting beside Vera.

'They'll heat up just as good in their cans, Maisie, and it saves bringing a pot, doesn't it?'

Maisie's the baby of our cottage. She looks like Shirley Temple without the curly hair. She's always got her arms out to be picked up and she lets you cuddle her for ages.

Vera gets the napkins and bottle of sauce ready. The first bread bun is in her hand.

'Let's have a sing-song while we're waiting. What about "Kum Bay Yah"?'

Sarah hands round the beakers of orange juice while we're singing. I want to drink it all but I'll have none left for my hot dog. When we've finished *Someone's praying, Lord, someone's crying, Lord*, and *someone's dying, Lord* the hot dogs are ready. Vera hands Sarah the empty bun, Sarah uses the fork to spear a hot dog, puts it straight in the bun and passes it back to Vera for the sauce. I'm finished mine by the time the last person's got theirs.

There's two full tins of hot dogs on the fire and they've got eight in each tin and there's loads of rolls of bread left in the bag. I think we might get another one.

'More orange juice?'

Sarah holds up the plastic bottle. I take my beaker over to her to be filled. Vera's nearly finished her hot dog. The fire sparks and hisses. Sarah wipes the edge of her mouth with her napkin.

'What about "Michael Row the Boat Ashore"?'

Vera nods because her mouth is full. The singing sounds nice in the darkness.

The hot dogs are bubbling in the can. Sarah uses two forks to move the tin to the edge of the fire.

'Who's for another hot dog?'

My hand shoots up. The second one lasts a bit longer. It's quiet while everyone's eating except for Vera humming 'Michael Row' to herself. I think about the presents we got for my ma and da yesterday in Ayr. Morag bought two small whisky glasses with a picture of Robert Burns on the front and she said one was for my ma and the other was for my da. I got a manicure set in a tartan case for my ma and an ashtray with a picture of the beach right in the middle that said *Greetings from Ayr* for my da. I was going to send them a postcard but I don't know our address. Vera said it wouldn't get to them with just *243 Wallace Street*. She said she had the proper address in our files back at the Homes but that wouldn't really be a postcard from Turnberry then, would it?

Vera starts singing 'Jesus Wants Me For a Sunbeam'. Malkey and Morag are the only ones not singing. Sarah says the best singers will get a prize and pulls two packets of Tunnock's caramel wafers out of the bag. The singing gets really loud. Malkey and Morag start mouthing the words but they're not really singing. Sarah still gives them a biscuit after everyone else has got theirs.

Vera pokes at the fire. Sarah tells us a ghost story about an old man who haunts the farm where she used to live. By the time she's finished the fire has died right down. We all have to get handfuls of sand and throw it on the fire. Malkey uses his feet to kick the sand over the fire. Sarah and Vera pack away the beakers and empty juice bottles. Morag helps me shake the blanket and roll it into a small bundle. Vera does her shouting thing until we are all in line for the walk home. Malkey holds the torch because Vera's carrying Maisie. If my da was here he'd give me a backy all the way home.

28

Shona pushes the meat around her plate. She's eaten the cabbage and the carrots and the potatoes. All that is left is seven grey lumps of stew. Vera watches her from the top of the table. She doesn't blink.

It used to be that Shona would chew at the meat and try to finish it but she never could. Vera would serve it up at teatime and then again at breakfast and Shona would cry her way through every meal until it was finished. Today, Shona isn't trying. She folds her arms and stares at the plate in front of her.

'You'd better make a start, young lady,' says Vera. 'You're not wasting perfectly good food in this house.'

Shona is a statue. Sarah starts to dish out the puddings. It's rice and Ribena. I'm glad there are no sultanas in the rice. Vera takes her own plate through to the kitchen. I can hear her telling Sarah that she'll *put a stop to this nonsense once and for all*.

Malkey elbows Shona in the head as he passes. 'It's no worth gettin in a *stew* aboot.'

I stop smiling when Shona wipes her eyes. Sarah and Vera come into the dining room. Vera speaks first.

'Right then, madam, if this is how you want it . . .'

Vera sticks a bit of stew onto the end of a fork and makes a grab for Shona's nose. As soon as Shona's hands go up to stop her, Sarah grabs them and holds them in her lap.

Shona looks like a goldfish. I swallow the giggle in my throat. The stew gets pushed into her open mouth. Her bottom lip starts to bleed where the fork has caught it. The lump is spat across the table. Vera slaps her hard on the side of the head and grabs her nose again. She manages to get two lumps into Shona's mouth and holds it tight shut.

'She won't be able to breathe,' says Sarah.

Vera stands behind Shona and tilts her head right back, holding her chin with both hands.

'Try and chew it, Shona,' says Sarah, hunched over her lap. 'You're nearly finished.'

Sarah is almost out of breath. Malkey sniggers as he takes his empty bowl into the kitchen.

'Ah'll hold her legs,' he offers, but Vera doesn't hear him.

The vomit is spectacular. Some of it gets caught in Vera's hair, the rest flies through the air like it's come out of a hose. It smells like vinegar. Gary Martin shoves his plate to one side. Splashes of sick sit on top of my rice.

'YOU FILTHY, DIRTY ANIMAL!' shouts Vera as Shona coughs and splutters the rest onto the floor. There's blood and sick and gravy and snotters and tears all over her face. Vera drags Shona out of the dining room by the hair.

Sarah starts to pick up the beakers and the overturned chairs. Some of her hair has come out of her clasp. Her hands shake as she wipes the milk off the floor.

'Finish your pudding,' she says to the other two tables.

Her voice is really quiet. She lets our table put their puddings in the bin. Malkey sits back in his chair and picks the meat out of his teeth with his fingernail.

29

The bottom stair creaks and I know it's him. There's only five stairs up to our room and the bottom one always makes that noise. I check that I still have my pants on underneath my pyjamas. I pull the blankets over my head and lie on my front. I think I'm breathing too loud.

His hands find my leg and move up to the waistband. I move around as if I might wake up but he waits until I'm still again. I tighten my whole body but I think he might feel it. His hands are on either side of me. My pyjama bottoms move across my bum like a see-saw.

I make some noise and move to the other side of the bed. I push the blankets back.

'Morag, ah need the toilet . . .' I rub at my eyes. My back is to Malkey. I walk over to Morag's bed and shake her shoulder. 'Ah need the toilet . . .' She doesn't move. By the time I turn round Malkey has gone.

30

When it rains we stand in the bus shelter until it passes, then go back to sitting on the wall. The bus driver is only dropping off one or two people every trip. I have my presents from Turnberry in my pocket.

'Ye never get many visitors when the weather's shite.'

Morag's right. The last few Saturdays have been the same. Things are mostly the same here but the weather can change everything, like when it's cold and you have to have porridge for breakfast or warm milk on your cereal or when it's nice and you have banana sandwiches and cake for tea and Vera lets you eat it outside on the grass like a picnic.

The days are always the same though; school every day, Saturday's pocket money, tuck shop then the bus stop for visitors. When we're older we'll be allowed to go into the village on a Saturday by ourselves and spend our pocket money. Sundays, service in the morning, five-mile walk in the afternoon (depending on the weather) and then the service in the evening.

Vera sends you up to the Drapery in the spring to get your summer clothes: shorts, T-shirts, nighties, sandals, new swimming costume, ankle socks, dresses and a special hat for Easter Sunday. In the autumn she sends you up for your winter clothes: cords or jeans, jumpers, tights, pyjamas.

When the weather's nice you can go to the park, queue up for the pedal boats on the pond, play down by the river, go on the trampoline in the sports hall, go swimming, play tennis or just play out. When it's cold you mostly stay inside and play board games, or read a book or draw a picture or colour in or watch the telly, except when it snows. Then you're out for ages, building snowmen and having snowball fights. Sometimes, when the weather's not good, they show Laurel and Hardy films on a Saturday morning up in the big main hall. I don't really like Laurel and Hardy.

Morag steps from puddle to puddle in her wellies. 'Fuck this, Puddin, if they don't come on the next bus ah'm off.'

In my first piano lesson Mr Shaugnessy shows me how to sit properly at the piano, back straight, not too near and not too far away. My feet can't reach the pedals, they dangle directly above them. My wrists have to be level with my arm. He says imagine there is a little fairy sleeping peacefully on your wrist. If you raise it too high she'll fall off, if you drop it too low she'll slide down.

Ten minutes pass and I still haven't played a note. Once he explains about the treble clef, middle C, the stave, time signatures, crotchets and semibreves, I'm ready to go. He makes me clap the rhythm of the notes first, and then I have to play them. He points at each note with his pencil. CCCC C— C— C— CCCC C— C— C—. I get it right first time. I move down to the next piece, which is almost the same except it has minims, two-beat notes. CCCC C-C- CCCC C-C- CCCC CCCC C-C- C—. Mr Shaugnessy claps his hands and smiles. He moves to the top of the piano and says we'll play it again but this time he'll join in. He counts four beats and then we are off. I don't lose my place and keep going to the end. The tune he plays on top makes the whole thing sound really good. He throws his head back when he gets to the end and does a fancy 'ripple' up the piano. I'm surprised he's so pleased about me playing one note but he is.

'A natural sense of rhythm, Ailsa . . . excellent stuff.'

He gives me homework to do on learning more notes and the musical alphabet, ABCDEFG. I have to do the next three exercises in the book. He pats me on the back as I leave the room.

'Well done, Ailsa, what an excellent start you've made.'

I go back the next day and give him the completed homework and play the three exercises in the book. He makes his eyes go big and smiles. I like it when he does that. It means he's pleased with me.

He shows me how to remember the notes on the treble clef; Every Good Boy Deserves Fun (line notes) and F A C E (for the space notes). He writes almost a full page of jumbled up notes in a brand new manuscript book and tells me that each set of jumbled up notes will spell a word. He does the first one for me, BADGE. I'm excited. I know I'll do it really well and get them all right. I can't wait to get home. The brand new manuscript book feels like treasure. Nobody else in Cottage 51 has music paper or piano books. I think I'll do the homework and then try and make up some words of my own that Mr Shaugnessy hasn't thought of and that will really impress him.

32

Morag doesn't want to join the choir. I tell her Mr Shaugnessy is really nice but she just laughs.

'Plum's a holy Joe,' she says, zipping up her anorak. 'Sittin at his organ . . . thumpin oot the hymns.' She mimics him playing but makes him look like a zombie.

They call him Plum because he looks like Professor Plum in Cluedo.

'The cunt gets aw blustery at school when ye don't sing properly.' Morag squeezes her feet into her shoes. She starts laughing. 'Me an Brenda wind the cunt up . . . We make these low moanin sounds when everybody else is singin an eventually he jumps up from behind the piano, the wee face bealin an the eyes aw angry.' She puts on a deep posh voice. '"Will whoever's making those ridiculous noises please stop it at once . . . it's spoiling the efforts of everyone else." Then Brenda wi a dead straight face turns tae look at the rest ay the class . . . "Ye better pack it in," she says. "Yer spoilin it fur the rest ay us."' Morag laughs quietly to herself then stamps her feet a couple of times to make sure her shoes are on properly. 'Funny as fuck, honest.'

It's probably better if I just go myself.

It's the first time I've been in the church other than a Sunday. It looks different. No flowers. None of the blue material with the gold crosses hanging from the pulpit. It's funny to think the church has a Sunday best just like us. The men in the choir are setting out the chairs. The women and older girls are standing around in small groups, laughing. I sit on one of the spare seats in the front row. Mr Shaugnessy is taking the heavy brown cover off the grand piano and opening the lid. It looks beautiful . . . the blackest, shiniest wood I've ever seen. It curves at the sides. I can see the reflection of my legs in the polish. They look fatter than they really are. I move them to check they are mine.

Everyone takes their seats, the children at the front and the adults at the back. I count twenty-one including me.

'We've been asked to sing at the end of the month at Barnard's Court Mission Hall in Greenock.' Mr Shaugnessy rubs both his hands together. 'So I thought we could do "All in the April Evening" and "Telephone to Glory".' The adults nod and begin to shuffle their music around. Mr Shaugnessy hands me a copy of the song and smiles straight at me.

The sounds coming from behind me are warm. I can't keep up with them for most of it and sometimes I just make my mouth move to the words without singing. It doesn't matter. Nobody tells me off. When I start to get the hang of the tune, it feels good to be part of the sound.

33

The minibus is leaving at six o'clock and Mr Shaugnessy said it wouldn't wait for stragglers. It's weird wearing school uniform on a Saturday night. I have on my best white socks that don't slide down and the shirt with the stiffer collar. Vera shouts 'Best behaviour' as I leave through the front door. The church bells ring the 'quarter to' tune. It feels good to be going somewhere different.

Maybe Greenock is beside Glasgow and maybe my ma has a friend in Greenock that she's visiting and maybe she'll bump right into me when I get off the bus and then she'll tell me that everything is sorted out now and she's allowed to take me home. She'll have a letter in her bag from the social worker and she'll show it to Mr Shaugnessy and he'll say, 'Excellent stuff, Mrs Dunn . . . wonderful news.'

My ma'll come in and listen to the singing and be really proud. Mr Shaugnessy will like my ma and shake her hand and then I'll go home.

All the children and most of the adults are already there when I arrive. Mr Shaugnessy's pale-blue Beetle pulls up and parks beside the minibus.

The minibus driver starts counting heads.

'We're going to need another car,' he says and looks around at the rest of the adults.

'The bus can take twelve, Mr Shaugnessy can take four . . .'

'I'll take mine,' says Mr Johnstone from Cottage 41.

The older girls make a dash for the minibus and pick their seats. Two house-parents get in the front. Mr

Shaugnessy points to the people nearest him and tells them to wait beside his car. I get to the front passenger door first. Two house-mothers and a quiet, older girl get in the back.

We drive through the main gates. The minibus follows behind. One of the house-mothers speaks to Mr Shaugnessy and asks about his wife and grandchildren. I look at the name signs of the towns we pass through, BRIDGE OF WEIR ... KILMALCOLM ... They don't look like Glasgow.

'Are you in good voice, Ailsa?'

It takes a second for me to realise that Mr Shaugnessy is talking to me. I nod and smile.

'I know all the words to "April Evening" off by heart,' I tell him. He makes his eyes go big and raises his eyebrows.

> *All in the April Evening*
> *April airs were abroad,*
> *The sheep with their little lambs*
> *Passed me by on the road,*
> *The sheep with their little lambs*
> *Passed me by on the road.*
> *All in the April Evening*
> *I thought of the Lamb of God.*

The women in the back give me a round of applause. Mr Shaugnessy chuckles in the front.

The Mission Hall smells of old hymn books and strong tea. There are no pictures on the walls, only words written in fancy letters with gold-edged paint: *His love endures forever ... Jesus is the light of the* world ... *You will know the truth and the truth will set you free.*

Rows of wooden chairs fill the main part of the hall. There is room to walk down the centre towards the small wooden stage. Two long tables are set against the back wall. Plates of cakes, sponges, biscuits, fruit bread and sandwiches fill one table. The teapots, cups, saucers, milk jugs and sugar bowls fill the other. The minister shakes hands with everyone as they come through the door. He is tall with thick white hair and dark eyebrows.

'Welcome, welcome, it's a pleasure to have you with us tonight.'

He sounds like Dr Finlay off the telly. The hall is mostly full of old women wearing neck scarves and brooches. A few of them still have their hats on; others are hanging up coats and fastening buttons on cardigans. Some of the older girls don't like the old people squeezing their arms or patting their heads. I don't mind. I like them taking my hand in theirs and asking my name and what age I am. 'Aren't you bonny,' they say. 'What lovely green eyes.'

The choir takes up the first three rows. I sit nearest the piano. The minister says how happy he is at the large turnout for the service and thanks all the women for the splendid contribution they've made to the 'tea'.

'We'll get the evening off to a rousing start with "When the Roll is Called up Yonder",' he says.

Mr Shaugnessy plays the introduction and everyone stands up. The old people like singing. Their heads are up and their feet are tapping.

The page on Mr Shaugnessy's music book keeps falling back on itself. He plays with one hand and tries to flatten the page with the other. It happens again. He makes some mistakes as he flicks at the page. I get up, stand beside him and hold the corner of the page in position. He smiles and carries on playing. When the hymn is finished he pats my arm.

'Well done, Ailsa, you saved the day.'

I go back to my chair and join the rest of the choir.

At the end of the service we are told to help ourselves to refreshments. Nobody counts how many cakes you have.

34

I can't sleep. It's Christmas Eve. The smells from the kitchen are making me hungry. I picture the Tiny Tears I put at the top of my list to Santa and wonder if he really will leave fewer presents for the bed-wetters.

There's giggling from the bedroom across the landing. Somebody's going to get put in the shed. Vera shouts from the bottom of the stairs, 'If you don't get to sleep, Santa won't come. I'll not tell you again.'

Silence.

The sitting-room door closes and a few soft whispers begin straight away.

No one has been allowed in Vera's sitting room for weeks. Malkey says it's because the presents are already there and there's no such thing as Santa Claus. I don't believe him. Malkey's a prick.

I need to go to the toilet again. To make sure. Even though I sit for a while, nothing comes. Morag's waiting for me when I get back.

'Whit else di ye put on yer list?' Her whisper is too loud.

'Tiny Tears, a pram, an etch-a-sketch an a paintin set.' I count them off in my hand.

'Well ah want a doll, a cradle, some clackers, a pair of roller skates an a selection box.'

Vera's in the kitchen. I can hear the oven door slam. The turkey is bigger than Ryan McCreedy and he's quite big for five. I hold my finger to my mouth to let Morag know to stay quiet.

Everything about Christmas is good: the songs in the church, making the Christmas cards in school, the pantomime in Glasgow, the paper chains we made to decorate the playroom. I made a cardboard angel with a ping-pong-ball head and Vera put it on the top of the Christmas tree.

My teacher, Miss Lockie, made us all bring in a sock to school. She hung them all across a line, which went diagonally from the edge of the blackboard to the wall behind her desk. She stuck a label on each one with our name on. At the end of every day she put a few more sweets in each stocking. It was nice to watch them get fatter. On the last day of school she handed them out and wished us all a merry Christmas. I love Miss Lockie.

Vera's back in her sitting room. I can hear the volume get louder on her telly.

'If ye need the toilet through the night, Ailsa, an yer scared, just wake me up, ah'll come wi ye.'

I nod quietly and turn over on my side.

35

Morag's bouncing on the bottom of my bed.

'Wake up,' she whispers. 'It's Christmas.'

I sit up in bed and rub at my eyes. It's dark. I can't tell if it's the middle of the night or not. My heart tightens while I feel the sheets and my pyjamas. It's hard to tell when the bed is warm. I have to get out of the bed, pull the covers back and wait for the cold. Morag moves her hand across the sheet.

'It's dry.'

I pat my pyjama bottoms and she's right, the material moves with me, it doesn't stick to my legs like it normally does. I might get the Tiny Tears. But then I'm thinking how would Santa know? Would he have to feel under the blankets? Would he sniff to check every bed?

'Everybody's awake,' says Morag. 'We're just waitin fur Vera.'

I can hear footsteps running across the landing and the sound of bodies jumping back into beds.

Vera's bedroom door opens. I can tell it's hers because the handle is loose and it makes that squeaky sound. Morag dives into her own bed and I quickly get under the covers. There is complete silence.

'Time to get up!' shouts Vera. 'Slippers and dressing gowns.'

She turns on lights as she comes to them. Within ten seconds everyone is on the landing. Vera stands at the bottom of the small set of stairs that separates our room from the other bedrooms.

'Be careful on the stairs and no pushing.'

She smiles and looks at us all. Ryan McCreedy squeals and jumps up and down. Vera turns to lead the way downstairs to the playroom. She is the Pied Piper.

The playroom door is locked. Vera takes a key from her dressing gown pocket and unlocks it.

'Santa will have left you a sack of toys each,' she says. The door is still shut. 'He's put your name on your sack so you don't touch anybody else's presents. Do you hear?'

Vera twists the door handle with one hand and finds the light switch with the other.

I can see white pillowcases stuffed with toys dotted around the room. I can see a bike and a scooter and a train set resting against some of the pillowcases. I can see Malkey's name and Ryan's name but I can't find my own name.

Morag shouts from the bottom end of the playroom.

'It's here, Ailsa. Yours is here!'

It's the pram I see first. Navy blue with silver writing on the side. The hood is up and the navy blue top cover is hooked to the sides with small black elastic hoops. I have to undo them to see what's inside.

She's almost hidden under the lacy quilted blanket and matching pillow. I pick her up. She smells of plastic and nylon and perfume. My arms are shaking. I don't want to put her down to check the rest of the pillowcase. I hold her tight to my chest so I can smell her hair. Morag is ripping the paper off her toys.

'Look, Morag, it's Tiny Tears.'

Morag is flicking through a *Bunty* annual then throws it to one side and rips at the paper of her next toy. I look around the playroom. Ryan McCreedy is sitting on his new bike, ringing the bell. Shona is putting red plastic pots on a white plastic cooker. The floor is covered in wrapping paper. Vera stands against the radiator watching everyone. She's yawning.

I take my dolly to show her.

'It's Tiny Tears,' I tell her. 'Ah got a Tiny Tears.'

She holds out her hands to have a look at it.

'She's beautiful, Ailsa,' she says. 'Santa must've been really pleased with you.'

She hands her back and I take her back to her pram. I fix the pillow and put the hood down so that she can sit up and watch me open the rest of my presents.

Morag's squeezing her foot into a roller skate. Her fingers move quickly but she can't seem to get the strap through the hole.

'Ah got the clackers an a Barbie an a selection box an a daft book . . .' she says. 'An ah've still got two presents tae open.'

I point to my pram and the Tiny Tears but she's too busy concentrating on the roller skates to look up.

36

We sit on the pavement and lean against the wall. Brenda Baxter swings backwards and forwards on a large iron gate. The sign on it says McGREGOR'S HOMES EPILEPTIC COLONY.

Morag starts laughing and points to Brenda.

'Hundreds of eppies've touched that gate ... you're gonnay catch whit they've goat.'

Brenda steps off the gate and pushes it away from her. She wipes her hands on her skirt and finds a space beside us against the wall.

'You're gonnay marry a colony,' says Brenda, 'wi big droopy lips an erms like a monkey.' She sticks her chin out and flaps her arms.

Morag stops laughing and elbows her in the ribs.

'Cheeky cunt,' she says, 'marry a colony.'

We sit in silence. Brenda rubs her side and Morag slowly tears the petals off a dandelion. I want to tell her that dandelions are 'pee the beds' and that she shouldn't really touch them but I decide not to. There are lots of things you don't tell Morag if you know what's good for you, like her new shoes for starting back at school next week. They make her walk like Frankenstein but she thinks they're great. I think about her walking down the aisle with her white dress and her big shoes and the colony walking beside her. I smile to myself.

'Ah'm gonnay marry Tom Jones an wear high heels every day.'

They're not listening. A colony opens the gate behind me and almost trips over my feet. He's wearing a white crash helmet with a black chinstrap.

'Let's follow im,' says Morag getting to her feet.

Brenda smiles and is soon in step with her. We pick up stones on the way. The colony is a few feet in front of them. He moves like a Thunderbird. I stay at the back because of what happened the last time.

A gang of us had been following one for ages. We were all singing 'Eppy, eppy, ugly git, eppy, eppy, huv a fit' when Morag grabbed me and pushed me straight into him. I had to hold onto his jacket to stop me from falling. His clothes smelled of medicine and vinegar. My legs felt like two pieces of rope. I couldn't get them to hold up straight. Morag laughed that big laugh of hers and everybody else joined in. I called her a *fuckin prick* and ran back to the cottage to tell on her. When she got in, she got sent to bed without any supper. Auntie Vera said that we should thank our lucky stars we didn't have what they had, and if she heard about any of us tormenting epileptics again, then she'd arrange for us to spend a night at the Colony.

We follow him through the main gates and down towards the post office. He starts to walk faster but we still keep up with him.

'Hey, Mister!' shouts Brenda. 'Tell us yer name.'

He doesn't answer.

'We only want tae talk tae ye.'

He puts his hands in his pockets and keeps on walking. She throws a stone at his helmet.

'If ye tell us yer name, we'll leave ye alane,' says Morag, walking alongside him.

He starts to run. Another stone bounces off his helmet.

'Fug ov, ya cunz.'

His voice is really loud, it sounds like a record set at the wrong speed. I look around. There's no one here. He's not very good at running. A couple of times it looks like he's going to fall over but he doesn't. We don't need to run to catch up with him; we just walk a lot faster.

'C'moan,' says Morag, 'just tell us yer name.'

He stops and turns around. We wait a few feet behind him. His face is shiny.

'Ma name's Zammy Verguson.'

He wipes the sweat from his eyes. We stand, not sure of what to do next. I feel ashamed. I think God's watching. He starts to repeat his name even louder, when his eyes begin to flicker and roll to the back of his head.

'He's gonnay huv a fit,' says Morag moving closer. Her eyes get bigger.

He sways a little, then drops to the ground. Two spoons fall from the inside of his jacket. We all move closer and bend over him, watching in silence. His whole body twitches and shakes. White spit froths at the side of his mouth.

'Fuckin freak,' says Morag quietly, not taking her eyes off him.

'Eppy cunt,' says Brenda, straightening herself up.

I drop my stones quietly onto the grass.

37

The dining room is dark, except for the light from the telly. A row of straight-backed grey chairs separates the TV area from the dining room. The three tables are set for breakfast. Bowls of dry cornflakes are covered with small white side plates. The younger ones are all in bed. The rest of us sit in front of the old black-and-white screen.

Malkey comes in just as the news starts. He punches the middle head. Gary Martin gives up his seat and sits on the floor. I'm glad I'm sitting at the end of the row.

Vera stands at the door.

'Bedtime.'

Gary and Ryan slide off their chairs and head up to bed.

Malkey sprawls across the empty seats. He checks the clock on the wall. 'You two should be in bed.'

'We're allowed,' says Mary. 'Auntie Vera says we can stay up to watch the horror.'

I know she only said it to annoy Morag, who got sent to bed straight after tea because she'd told her teacher to *fuck off* and threw a chair across the classroom. I thought about just going to bed at my normal time so Morag wouldn't be left out but I really want to watch the horror movie. If Malkey complains, Vera might change her mind so I don't move or make a sound. I can hear her footsteps coming down the stairs and the door of her sitting room clicking shut.

Malkey tuts. 'Well ye better be fuckin quiet, ah'm warnin ye.'

The news goes on forever, then there's *Late Call* for another five minutes, Eventually, the film begins.

It's thunder and lightning. Only one window of the castle is lit. An old man tightens the straps around the legs of a body on the table. The old man stands beside a lever and holds it with both hands. He presses it down hard. The lights flicker and almost go out. The monster doesn't look that scary when he's lying on the table. Mary gets herself a bit closer to me on the chair.

Frankenstein breaks free from the straps and steps off the table. Mary giggles and gets closer. I think of Morag and her big shoes. *The monster smashes the door of the lab and disappears into the night.* We stare at the screen in front of us. The right side of my body is warm from sitting so close to Mary. It makes me feel less scared.

The monster has killed a villager. A professor and two policemen arrive at the castle and find the laboratory. Mary slides her hand down to poke me in the leg. I look at her. She tilts her head and moves her eyes in Malkey's direction at the same time. He's not watching the telly, he's got his willy in his hand and he's pulling it backwards and forwards. He's really gentle with himself.

A beautiful baroness sits at her dressing table, brushing her hair. Frankenstein steps up behind her. She sees his reflection in the mirror and screams. The monster looks puzzled. Mary nudges me again to have another look. I don't want to. She giggles and I can see his head turn in our direction out of the corner of my eye. I wish she'd stop giggling; it's making him think we want him to do it. His feet smell. I move to the edge of the chairs and cover my nose with my hand. I pick at the insides. The snotter is rubbed into a small, perfect round ball.

The villagers are carrying torches. They head for the church. The professor and the policemen ride ahead on horseback.

'D'ye want tae touch it?'

The rubbing is getting quicker. Malkey's legs stiffen and his toes twitch against Mary's leg.

'Ah'll rub you as well, ye'll really like it.'

He pulls his pyjamas down to just above his knees.

'C'mon, lassies, huv a wee feel, it's throbbin like fuck.'

Mary giggles again. I elbow her really hard. She can be really stupid sometimes. If she doesn't pack it in he'll come over and do it in front of us. She thinks it's a big joke because he doesn't come to her bed in the middle of the night and put his hands under her blankets. She doesn't know that he's not scared of staying in your room for ages until he thinks you're sleeping again. He doesn't go near Mary so she's alright.

His breathing is getting louder. He's making little moaning sounds. His arm stops moving.

The monster is dead. He lies across the steps of the church. The professor is holding the pistol that shot him.

We don't wait for the music at the end. I quickly follow Mary out of the dining room. As I pass Malkey's bowl, I lift the plate and flick the snotter into his cornflakes. We take the stairs two at a time.

38

Miss Lockie stands at the front of the class. Her cheeks are red. She's wearing her nice blue jumper. It's my favourite.

'Has anyone noticed that spring is almost upon us?' she asks. Loads of hands shoot up. I don't really know what I'm supposed to have noticed.

'Catherine,' says Miss Lockie.

'There's no more snow, Miss.'

'That's right, Catherine, the weather is becoming milder.' Arms are stretched even higher as Miss Lockie looks around the room. I wish I could think of something.

'Andrew, what do you think?'

Andrew Muir clears his throat. He speaks quietly. 'Snowdrops, Miss.'

Rab Kennedy giggles behind his hand and Jimmy Milligan says, *Snowdrops! Snowdrops!* in a really high voice.

'You're absolutely right,' says Miss Lockie, staring at Rab and Jimmy.

This makes them stop.

'We shall probably see some crocuses and daffodils too in the next few weeks.'

She picks up a book from her desk and reads a poem about trees, where the leaves speak to each other and they do a trick every year by coming alive again. It sounds like a song.

'Spring is about change,' says Miss Lockie. 'Rebirth, renewal.' She writes these words on the blackboard. 'And because it is a very important season, we are going to write a poem about it and enter your poems in the school poetry competition.'

We have to make a list of words that remind us of spring. Once Miss Lockie has checked our list, we can begin our poem. It's harder than I thought, I can only think of nine words:

Snowdrops
Buds
Leaves
Sunshine
Lambs
Squirrels
Flowers
Worms
Easter eggs

'Very good, Ailsa, you may begin,' says Miss Lockie, and I turn to a clean page in my book.

I want to write about a squirrel that wakes up after the winter and everything is better but a lot of the words are harder to rhyme than I thought. Miss Lockie says we only need to do one verse but I want to write two. Marjorie shows me hers.

Spring flowers are nice
There's no more ice
Lams have little legs
I will get Easter Eggs

I tell her about the 'b' in 'lambs'. She starts humming while she draws a sun and some flowers at the bottom of her page. It nearly puts me off. I finish the second verse and take it over to Miss Lockie's desk. She reads it.

THE SQUIRREL

I am asleep
When I wake up it will be warm
My eyes will peep
To make sure there is not a storm
I will sing
And wake up all my family
'Get up it's spring'
And they will stand beside me.

Miss Lockie is smiling.
'This is a very good poem, Ailsa, well done.'
She reads mine and Andrew's out to the rest of the class. His is about a tree putting its clothes back on. I think his might win. Jimmy Milligan says, *Get up it's spring* in his high voice again and Miss Lockie makes him stand in the corridor. He'll get the belt. I'm glad. She collects in all the poems then walks us to the cloakroom. The bell goes off for playtime.

39

'What're ye wearin knickers fur? Ye know she'll go mad.'

My eyes won't open properly; the light in the bedroom hurts them. I can hear Vera's Scholls on the stairs. Sometimes you can get past her if she's busy.

'Ye better hide them knickers in the sheets ... yer gonnay get killed.'

Morag only wets the bed sometimes. I wet it every day.

'Don't just stand there like a dummy, fuckin move!'

The tears come easily.

'Nae point in greetin,' she says. 'C'moan, ah'll help ye.'

Morag pulls the covers back and loosens the corners of the sheets. I step out of the pyjamas and the knickers. She starts to wrap the sheets into a ball then places the bundle in front of me. I drop the knickers into the pile. She wraps the rest of the sheets and puts them on top of my pyjamas.

'Malkey Donnelly keeps comin intae the room, Morag, an he keeps tryin tae touch us.'

A big bubble snotter comes out of my nose. My eyes are really nipping.

'He puts his hands under the blankets and pulls ma pyjamas doon.'

Morag stops checking the blankets.

'Naebody'll swap beds wi me an even though ah tuck the blankets in really tight he always gets them loose ... ah want tae go hame, Morag, ah don't like it here.'

'Dirty cunt,' says Morag.

She puts her arm round my shoulder.

'Ye kin sleep wi me, Ailsa. Don't worry, he'll no get ye.'

40

The note says *Please excuse Ailsa's late arrival at school today. She had an appointment with the doctor about her bed-wetting.* The classroom is empty. They must have gone to assembly. I rip the note into tiny pieces and hide it under some papers in the bin. I walk down the corridor to the main hall. If anyone asks, I'll tell them I slept in.

Mrs Carmichael stands guard at the doors. She holds a finger to her lips and opens the door gently. The lines around her mouth have lipstick in them. I find my seat beside Marjorie.

I'm glad the note's in the bin. I told the doctor about my dream; where I'm sitting on the toilet and it's alright to 'go' and how I wake up after that with my sheets all wet and pyjamas soaking. He said, *Mmm* and wrote something in his notes. He's given me a box with a bell in it that's attached to some wires and a brown rubber mat. As soon as the mat gets wet, the bell goes off. It's not fair. I'm not the only one who wets the bed. There are others in the bathroom with me in the mornings, washing the sheets and putting them through the wringer. It's better when there's two to hang them out. They're heavy and twisted and as big as a parachute.

I know that's why I'm not allowed drinks after six o'clock and why Vera stands over me while I have a pee but I'm not the only one. Vera told the doctor I was the worst. I don't want a box with a bell . . .

'Today's assembly is a very special one,' says Mr Bennett. His voice is low and deep. He jingles the change in his pocket as he walks across the front of the hall. 'Today we will announce the winner of our poetry competition.'

Chairs scrape across the wooden floor. Mr Bennett waits until the murmuring stops and the hall is quiet.

'The older students were awarded their prizes yesterday,' he continues, 'and I have to say, the standard was particularly high.'

The teachers all nod behind him. Miss Lockie is smiling. I'd forgotten about the poem. It feels more important now than it did in the classroom. I lean forward in my chair.

'The winning poem took a very unusual view of the spring season', he says. 'We liked the idea of . . .'

Mr Bennett always talks a lot in assemblies. It's usually about the countries he visited when he was an officer in the Navy. I don't think my poem had an unusual view of spring.

Marjorie is clapping, everyone is. I can see Andrew Muir shaking hands with the Headmaster. He collects his certificate and an enormous gold-wrapped Easter egg. Frances McAfferty from the class above me gets second prize and the hall goes quiet again.

'Our third and final prize was awarded for a poem we all agreed was thoughtful and caring . . .' This is worse than the doctor's, worse than the box. 'So it gives me great pleasure to ask Ailsa Dunn from primary six to come forward and collect her certificate.'

Marjorie nudges me. I pull up my socks and walk to the front of the hall. I can hear Jimmy Milligan hissing, *Get up it's spring* but I don't care.

41

Morag can skip for hours. I don't like skipping. It makes me feel fat. My fringe is sticking to my head and the collar of my school shirt is beginning to rub against my neck. Morag tells me not to look at my feet. We're doing doubles but I can't last more than five swings of the rope.

'Take over from Brenda,' says Morag, after my legs get caught in the ropes again. I take the wooden handle. Brenda kicks her shoes off. They get up to fifteen before Brenda gets out of time.

'She's too slow, Morag,' says Brenda. 'Let's just play singles and see who can skip the most.'

I take off my jumper and sit on the grass. Morag goes first. I stop counting after twenty-two. I can see Malkey coming down the road. His hands are in his pockets and his shoulders are swinging from side to side. He looks like a skittle. He's been to the Emergency Dentist in the village. His face was all puffed up at dinnertime and Vera said he had an abscess.

'Ooyhh!' shouts Malkey.

Morag keeps skipping. I pull at the grass next to me.

'C'mere, Ailsa,' he shouts. I pretend I can't hear him. 'I've got a surprise fur ye.'

My pile of grass gets bigger.

'Fuck off!' Morag shouts at him.

I think she's up to forty-seven.

'Please yersel,' shrugs Malkey. 'It wis somethin aboot yer da, but never mind.'

He spits at her feet. It just misses her by an inch. Her legs get caught in the ropes.

'Whit aboot ma da?' she shouts after him.

'Aw ye want tae know noo? Ah'll tell Ailsa.'

He stands behind the bush at the side of our cottage, watching to see if I'll follow.

'Go an find oot whit he's on aboot,' says Morag, 'an ah'll come roon in a minute tae check he's no bein funny.'

I don't want to go, Malkey's stronger than Morag and the smell of his spot cream makes me feel sick. Morag pushes me forward. I can hear the skipping ropes slapping at the ground.

Malkey's nose and chin are shiny with sweat. There's dried blood at the edges of his mouth. I glance at his trousers.

'Hurry up,' he shouts, 'or ah'm goin.'

I stand beside him. He puts one hand round my shoulder and the other one next to my ear. His lips touch my skin. I'm not sure if I've heard him right, I think he's lying but I don't know.

Morag's behind me. 'Whit did he say?'

I look at Malkey.

'Go on,' he says. 'It's true.'

I start to run. Morag's beside me in seconds.

'He says he saw my da at the bus stop . . . he was being sick . . . said he looked a bit drunk.'

She takes off ahead of me.

'Wait.'

I can hear Malkey laughing behind me. By the time I get to the bus stop, Morag's holding my da's hand. He's wiping his mouth with the sleeve of his free arm.

'Aw, Puddin!' he shouts, holding his hand out.

He rubs my head while I squeeze both arms round his waist. My cheek is pressed against the buckle of his belt but it doesn't hurt. His trousers smell a little bit.

I try to think of all the questions I promised myself I'd ask him but I can't remember any of them and anyway, he looks different. There's a small scar on his top lip and his nose seems wider. I'm angry with myself that I've forgotten what my own da looks like. His voice is the same.

'Jesus Christ, ye both got big,' he says, patting my back.

'I'm nine, Da, in two weeks' time.'

'Fer fucksake, Puddin, nine? Yer never nine, are ye?

He looks at me like I'm telling him a lie.

'In two weeks, Da, July the third.'

I drop my hands from around his waist and find his free hand. I don't know what I like best, looking at him or cuddling him. I stare at him, hoping that this time the pictures in my head last longer than before.

'Will you an my ma come back in two weeks, da?

He cannot hear me. Morag's telling him about all the fights she's won and how she's the hardest girl in her year.

My da squeezes her shoulder. 'You stick up fur yersel, hen,' he says, 'don't let any ah these cunts get the better of ye.'

She smiles and covers her mouth with her hand.

Vera brings a tray of tea into the playroom. There's some shortbread and iced ginger cake on the plate.

'It's nice to see you again, Miss Chambers, you look younger every time I see ye.'

Vera smiles and stays to pour out the tea.

'It's been quite a while,' says Vera, 'but it's nice to see you too, Mr Dunn.'

'Call me Frankie,' says my da, 'all the best people do.'

'Where's my ma?' asks Morag.

This gets rid of Vera and stops my da smiling at her.

'She's no well, hen, a touch of flu.'

Morag starts showing my da all the punches she gave Katrina McGee last week. I have to be Katrina. My da is slapping his knee.

'C'mon, Paddy,' he says, 'give her what for.'

Vera comes back in the playroom. We both jump up.

'They were showin me their wrestlin, Miss Chambers, Giant Haystacks and Big Daddy.'

'Well I just brought this through to let you see how well one of your daughters is doing at school.'

Vera hands my da the framed poetry certificate. I can't stop smiling. I quickly do the poem in my head to check that I still remember it.

'My oh my,' says my da. 'Third prize in the primary school poetry competition.'

His finger follows the writing on the certificate. Morag gets up and does a handstand against the wall.

'I can tell you the poem, Da, I remember it . . . all of it.'

'DEFINENTLY,' says my da. 'This ah've got to hear.'

I clear my throat and make up my mind to do it really slow so that he looks at me longer than he did Morag.

' "The Squirrel" by Ailsa Dunn.'

My da smiles.

' "I am asleep. When I wake up it will be warm . . ." '

'Bloody marvellous,' he says when I get to the end.

He's clapping his hands and whistling through his fingers.

'Ye should've won first prize, Puddin, fur that wee poem.'

I sit down beside him. He cuddles me hard.

'Huv ye heard this one?' he asks. ' "There was a young man from Caerphilly . . ." '

42

He's back. I can hear him on the stairs. I get out of bed as quietly as I can and slide in beside Morag. I shake her to wake her up.

'He's back, Morag.'

She wakes up as the bedroom door opens. Malkey tiptoes towards my bed. I shut my eyes tight so he won't see me.

'AUNTIE VERARRRRR!'

The shouting is really loud. Malkey is frozen.

'AUNTIE VERARRRRR!'

He's out the door before she's finished shouting. A few seconds later I can hear the springs squeak on his bed.

'What's all this noise?' Vera thumps across the landing.

I move back to my own bed and stick my head under the blankets. Vera barges through the door and sticks the light on.

'What's all the shouting about?'

Morag rubs at her eyes.

'Ah thought there wis somebody in the room, there wis a big shadow at the door.'

'A shadow? I'll give you bloody shadows, young lady. Get straight back to sleep and don't let me hear another peep out of you.'

Vera flicks the switch off and closes the door. She thumps her way down our set of stairs and up her own. I can hear her going into the boys' rooms to check they're all sleeping.

'That'll fuckin teach him, eh, Puddin?'

Morag's not scared of anybody.

43

The music room is locked. I chap on the door and try the handle again. Nothing. Mr Shaugnessy's car is parked outside the main hall so I know he can't be far.

He's probably down in the kitchen, making the tea. I take my English book with me to show him the story and the gold star. Mr Shaugnessy'll like it because it's about the Mission Hall in Greenock. Miss Lockie said she loved it because she could smell the scones and the tea brewing and she could see all the old ladies in their hats and scarves and she could feel how cold it was getting back into the minibus at the end of the night. She read it out to the whole class and then held up the book to show them the star at the bottom. Miss Lockie's my favourite teacher after Mr Shaugnessy.

The kitchen is at the back of the main hall. There's a sink and a cooker and cupboards along the other wall. The wooden shutter is pulled down but when it's up you can serve people in the main hall at concerts and sometimes the film shows on a Saturday morning.

The kitchen door is shut and I know before I open it there's no one inside. I walk to the other end of the hall and check the backstage door that leads to the nearest toilets but it's locked as well. Sometimes there's a cleaner wandering around, pushing a flat, dry mop across the wooden floor, or you can hear Mr Wilkie whistling while he stacks up chairs at the back of the hall or sets them out in nice neat rows. There's no one around today.

I go down the first set of stairs that face the front of the building and lean forward at the window to check that his car is still there. It hasn't moved. I try the music room again but it's still locked. I don't want to wait on the stairs outside the music room. It's too dark. But if I go into the main hall and play the piano, he'll hear me when he comes back and he'll know I'm there.

It sits in the corner of the hall, to the side of the stage. It's a grand piano, like the one in church, but it's scratched, and the pedal squeaks when you press it and some of the lower keys stick when you play them.

I play my best tunes first and then some scales. And then I play chopsticks and the theme tune from *Z Cars* and then I hold the pedal down with my foot and press as many keys as I can with both hands flattened out and listen to the mushed up sounds they make. Mr Shaugnessy doesn't like you doing that to the piano, so I only do it once, but even when I take my foot off the pedal it doesn't clear all of the sounds and they hang in the air for ages afterwards.

I climb onto the window sill and have a look outside. I can see Cottage 3 and 8 and 6 and 4 and the roof of Cottage 5. A boy's got a bike turned upside down in the yard of Cottage 6 and he's pulling at one of the wheels. A cottage auntie takes washing off the line outside Cottage 4 and puts it into a red plastic basket. She sticks the clothes pegs into a clothes-hanger holder like the ones that some of the bigger girls make at school. Mary made the one that hangs on our washing line. A gardener, in green overalls, walks slowly round the edges of the flower-bed that sits in the middle of the large green square between the houses, tidying the edges with big two-handled scissors. I watch him until he's finished. The flowerbed looks nice.

I go back to the piano and play my two best pieces again. A creaking sound from the gallery makes me stop and look up from the piano. It's dark at the back of the gallery; you can see the first couple of rows of seats but nothing else. The small window for the projector is just a black square. I stare at it for ages but nothing moves. It wasn't a little creak, it was a big creak.

Maybe the something that's up there is hiding behind the chairs, right at the back. Maybe it's waiting for the music to start again so it can creep out the side door, come down the stairs and get me in the main hall. My fingers play a C major scale while my eyes fix on the side door. I play the scale at least ten times but the side door doesn't move, not even a little bit.

Maybe it can see me watching and won't make its move until I turn away. Maybe it's waiting for me to be busy again.

I know what to do. I'll play the Mozart, which I know by heart, and I'll look at my fingers and everywhere else except the gallery and then, when it's least expecting it, I'll turn round really quick and catch it and if I see it going towards the door I'll run.

I start the Mozart and look at the window in front of me. I look down at my fingers and then at the stage curtains. They begin to move like they're breathing. I check the curtains at the windows; they don't budge. I look back at the stage. The curtains are still moving; slowly, silently.

I can't work out how it moved from the gallery to behind the curtains. Maybe it made itself invisible and sneaked under the crack of the side door and whooshed down the stairs and round the building and then came in the same door as me and crept up the stairs to the stage door and made itself fit under the gap at the bottom of the stage door and it's now behind the curtains, getting bigger and bigger. Maybe it's holding its arms out in front of itself, getting ready to pounce, and its fingers are getting longer and sharper and its mouth is starting to open so it can get me. It'll definitely get me because I'm jammed in the corner of the hall by the piano.

My chest is trying to get out of my skin.

The kitchen door clicks at the other end of the hall and I'm up on my feet. My body won't move fast enough. I pick up my English book and run out of the hall. I hold onto the banister while my feet take the stairs two at a time. The top half of my body is tight and hard but my legs are two giant balls of knitting wool.

Outside, on the path, my feet slow down to a quick walk. I catch up with two house-parents in front of me. The man is doing all the talking, the woman has her hands in her pockets and her head is down. I keep myself a few paces behind them. The sounds of their feet and his voice start to calm me down.

Through the small space between the couple in front of me, I can see Mr Shaugnessy walking towards me. He has a small carrier bag in his hand. I step from behind the couple. Mr Shaugnessy smiles and holds up the carrier bag.

'Supplies, Ailsa, we can't do without our tea and biscuits, eh?' He puts the carrier bag down, takes his hat off and wipes at his head with a hankie.

'Ah canny help ye the night, Mr Shaugnessy. Ah've got tae go an see the nurse fur a check-up fur ma ears an Auntie Vera says ah wisny tae be late or ah'd get inty trouble.'

Mr Shaugnessy folds the hankie back up and puts it into his pocket.

'Not a problem, Ailsa. You carry on. There's nothing

that won't keep until tomorrow.' Mr Shaugnessy puts his hat back on, picks up the carrier bag and walks slowly towards the main hall.

I pass the flowerbed with the trimmed edges. The gardener's done a good job.

44

Malkey never gives me peace to practise. If he comes into the playroom when I'm in the middle of practising I might as well stop. There's no point trying to go on. He especially loves tormenting me with the piano lid, doing the whole I'm just walking past, minding my own business thing, and then flicking at the lid to get it to slam on my fingers.

He's nearly caught me a couple of times, mostly when I'm in the bubble. It's the best thing about playing the piano, the way it shuts everything else out. It slowly surrounds you, the noises on the outside start to disappear until you can't hear the other kids anymore. It's just you and the notes and the sounds. Practising feels like being a painter. Each new piece or section feels like you have a blank canvas in front of you and learning the notes is like sketching the outline. I make myself smile sometimes because I picture myself sitting at the piano wearing a beret and an artist's smock. Sometimes I have a moustache and sometimes I don't.

The music in front of me is the palette and the sounds I make are the painting. When I stop to correct mistakes or practise a run of notes until they're perfect I imagine I'm the painter, standing back, dabbing at the canvas. I want to make noises like a Frenchman but I stop myself. They think I'm weird as it is. Derek says it's only *freaks* that want to play an instrument. He says *it wouldnae be so bad if you could play somethin from the charts but aw the Mozart shite's just rubbish*. In my head I say *Vwala* when I'm happy with it and that's good enough.

But the bubble works too well sometimes; you don't see or hear Malkey until the piano lid almost traps your fingers.

The worst time was when he sent Ryan McCreedy over to do it. Ryan was being all cocky because he had Malkey to protect him and wasn't the least bit frightened of the look I was trying to give him. Malkey loved it, he kept saying, *Go on, Ryan, kick fuck ooty the music stool*. And Ryan would wait till you were playing and take a run at it. I knew he had to go along with Malkey even if he didn't want to, but if I'd been able to get a hold of him I'd have battered him stupid, Malkey or not.

With Malkey it's best if you just stop altogether and go and do something else until he gets bored and goes off to watch telly or decides to pick on someone else.

I used to sit at the piano with my hands in my lap waiting for him to go but that just started him off on the flicking rolled-up bits of paper or picking his nose and flicking that when he wasn't getting the reaction he wanted. There's no point telling Vera because she only says, *Pack it in, Malcolm*, like she's reminding him to brush his teeth or tuck his shirt in, but Malkey always gets you back if you tell on him.

The latest thing is banging on the keys really hard with his fists to put me off as much as possible when I'm trying to play. Sometimes, when I know he's in the shed doing the potatoes, I play the same scale up and down and up and down about ten times, then I move onto the next scale and do the same. I can play scales all night. I'm really good at scales. I keep it up until I hear the tap on full for the final rinse of the potatoes then I put my books away and close the lid of the piano. He's not the only one who's good at tormenting.

45

Ryan McCreedy's going to end up getting battered. He won't move along to let Malkey get in to watch the film. He's sticking his elbows out to keep a bit of space around him but Malkey's getting annoyed. He stands in front of him, blocking the telly. Ryan has his head down. His ears are bright red.

'Get yer fuckin elbows oot the way or ah'll kick yer cunt in.'

Ryan moves them a tiny bit. His head's still down but his eyes are trying to see what Malkey is going to do.

'This is yer last warnin, McCreedy, keep yer elbows like that an see whit happens.'

Vera let us come in because it was raining. She said we could watch the Saturday afternoon film as long as there was no carry-on. We'll end up getting sent out again if there's any fighting.

'Right then.' Malkey grabs him by the neck and throws him off the seats. He takes the space that Ryan had. Tony Curtis walks into the circus tent with a jacket covering his dummy hand. He watches his friends on the trapeze.

'Get aff ma seat,' says Ryan, pulling at Malkey's jumper. The jumper moves but Malkey doesn't. He's breathing hard. 'Get aff ma fuckin seat.'

Malkey punches him hard in the chest. Ryan drops down to his knees. He can't get his breath. His head and chest move like he's taking in deep breaths but nothing seems to be going in or out. The doorbell rings. Ryan's hands start grabbing at the legs nearest him. His chest starts to make dragging, droning sounds and he stops moving around and concentrates on his breaths.

Vera opens the dining room-door. 'Morag, Ailsa.' She leaves the door open for us.

Ryan pulls himself up into the space I've left. He leans forward with his head in his hands and takes long deep breaths. We head out into the hall. My ma's pushing the wet hair off her face and pulling at her coat to shake the rain off.

Vera opens the playroom door.

'I'll stick the kettle on, Mrs Dunn. Morag can sort you out with a nice cup of tea.'

We follow my ma over to the seats beside the window. She takes her coat off and puts it on the back of one of the chairs.

'Fucksake, lassies. Look at the size ay ye.' She pulls us both into her. I put my arms around her waist and squeeze. Morag doesn't cuddle her properly. She leans against her but keeps her arms at her side.

'Ye've lost aw yer baby teeth, Ailsa. Yer smile looks different.' She runs her hand across my hair. Morag steps back and leans against the table. My ma strokes her arm.

'Yer nearly as big as me, Morag. Whit are they feedin ye? Magic beans?'

Morag likes that. She makes out she's rubbing something off her nose but she's trying to hide her smile. We sit by the window. My ma gets her fags out of her pocket. Morag runs to the kitchen to get her an ashtray. I don't know what to do. I feel too big to sit on her knee but I want to. I move closer to her.

'C'mere, hen, let me get a proper look at ye.' I stand in front of her. She squeezes my hand. Her fingers work their way between my fingers. Morag puts the ashtray down on the table.

'Fucksake, ah nearly forgot.'

She puts her fag in the ashtray and feels around in her pockets. She takes out a little pink-and-white-striped bag. It's too little for sweets. She lifts out two silver necklaces that are tangled up with each other. Morag moves closer. The smoke is getting in my ma's eyes. She moves the ashtray out of the way. She manages to separate them and hands us one each. There's a little silver disc on the end of the chain. It has funny marks on it.

'Ah've seen these, Ma – ma pal's got one. Ye spin the disc bit and it says *I love you*.'

Morag unhooks the back and tries to put hers on. My ma smiles. I spin it and she's right. It does say *I love you*.

'Pass it here, Puddin, an ah'll put it on fur ye.'

I hold my hair up. I like the feel of my ma's hands at the back of my neck. Morag is getting annoyed with herself. She cannot get hers on. My ma pats my shoulder to let me know it's on and gets up to help Morag. I hold the disc out in front of me and spin it. It's a real necklace, made of real silver, not one of those elastic strings with beads on. Wait till the rest of them see what we've got.

Morag slides the disc from side to side on the chain.

'Ye like them then, eh?' My ma picks up the fag from the ashtray. It's burnt down to the end. I sit on her knee and hold the necklace out for her to look at.

'Look, Ma.' Morag is at the piano. 'I can lift this right aff the ground.'

Morag's face is all twisted with the effort of it.

'Jesus Christ, Morag, watch yersel.' My ma gets up to help her but she places it back down with only a small thud. My ma puts her hand at her chest and keeps it there.

'Fucksake, Morag, ye nearly gave me a heart attack.'

Morag smiles. 'Ah could lift you, ma, ah kin lift lots a people.'

My Ma starts laughing. 'Whit're ye like, Paddy?' Before she can turn to go back to her seat, Morag has a hold of her with both hands just under her bum. My ma wobbles a bit as her feet leave the ground and she puts her arms on Morag's shoulders.

'Fucksake, Morag, whit're ye playin at?' My ma can't do anything for laughing. I put my arms out in case Morag drops her. This makes my ma laugh even more.

'Put me doon, Morag!' My ma's skirt is pulled up at the back. Morag's face is beetroot. She takes a few steps to prove she really is strong before she puts my ma back down on the ground.

'Fucksake, Paddy, yer strong right enough.' My ma fixes the back of her skirt. Morag smiles and puts the chain back in her mouth and slides the disc from side to side. My ma sits back down at the window and lights up another fag.

'Must be aw the dinners they feed ye, eh?'

Morag nods and leans against the table beside my ma.

'Are ye better noo, Ma? Are we goin hame?'

My ma turns to me and the smile leaves her face. She flicks her ash into the ashtray.

'Soon, lassies, ah've only got a few things tae sort oot wi the social workers.'

Morag moves to the other side of the table.

'How long is soon, Ma?'

My ma goes quiet and twirls the end of the fag in the ashtray.

'It's up tae the social workers, Ailsa, but ah'm on the list fur a bigger hoose an as soon as ah get that, ah think they'll let ye come back.'

Morag kicks the bottom of the table leg. Her voice is

quiet. 'Where's ma da?' How come he hasny come doon wi ye?' She doesn't look at my ma. She stares at her feet.

'He's no well, Morag, a touch ay the flu or somethin.'

Morag carries on kicking at the table leg.

'Will ye come back tae visit, Ma, while yer waitin fur the hoose?'

My ma pulls me closer to her. 'Nae bother, Puddin. Come hell or high water, eh?'

Vera comes into the playroom, holding a tray. 'This'll warm you up, Mrs Dunn.' She puts the tray on the table. 'Just help yourself, there's plenty more where that came from.'

My ma says 'Thanks' and starts sorting out the milk and sugar in her cup. Vera stands for a few seconds but my ma carries on sorting out the tea. Vera shuts the door hard behind her.

'So whit's that Vera like then,' says my ma, pouring the tea into her cup.

I look at Morag. Morag doesn't say anything. My ma looks at me. I look at Morag again.

'She's a moanin-faced cunt. They're aw moanin-faced cunts.'

My ma smiles and shakes her head. Her fingers play with the soft part of my ear.

'An Ailsa's nae better, she's a right clipe, always tryin tae get ye inty trouble.'

I stare at Morag. I'm waiting for her to start laughing and say she's only kidding. She doesn't laugh. She stares at me like it's true.

My ma puts the cup back on the saucer. 'Ye've got tae stick the gither, lassies, help each other oot.'

Morag's trying to get me into trouble with my ma.

'Ah don't clipe on er, Ma. Ah never clipe on er.' The tears are hot. My ma cuddles me. I can smell the warmth of her jumper.

'C'mere, Morag.' My ma puts her arm out to bring her into the cuddle. Morag moves towards my ma.

The punch she throws lands on the side of my head. My hand goes up to the spot.

'Pack it in, Paddy!' shouts my ma. She skelps Morag hard on the arm.

'Yer a sooky wee cunt,' shouts Morag and goes over to sit on the window sill furthest away from the table. She wraps herself in the curtain.

My ma rubs the side of my head and gets up to talk to her.

'Ye canny be lashin oot at the wain like that. Fer fucksake, Paddy, ye don't know yer ain bloody strength.'

'Whit dae you care?'

My ma gives up after a few minutes. She sits back down and puts her head in both of her hands. I put my arm around my ma's shoulders. I hate Morag. She spoils everything.

My face feels tight where the tears have dried. The only sound in the room is Morag sniffing. After a while my ma sits up and lights another fag. I get my old school book out of my locker and show my ma the three silver stars and the four gold stars. She flicks through the pages slowly and reads some of the stories.

'Look at yer neat handwritin, Ailsa, it's lovely.' My ma gets up and takes her coat off the back of the chair.

'Ah'll huv tae get back fur yer da, lassies, make sure he's awright.'

Morag doesn't move from the window sill but the sniffing's stopped.

'Ye kin keep the book, Ma, an let ma da see it.'

Her eyes fill up. Her voice is shaky. 'He'll like that, Puddin, an ah kin read it properly on the bus.' She bends down and holds me for ages. Her hair smells beautiful.

While she buttons her coat, I look in my locker to see if

there's anything else she would like. There's only felt pens and a Cindy and some books.

'This is great, Puddin, yer da'll be made up wi this.'

Morag still doesn't move.

'Ah'm goin, Morag. Come an walk me tae the bus stop.'

The curtain doesn't move.

'At least come an say cheerio.'

My ma waits for a few seconds then she takes my hand and I walk her up to the bus stop.

46

Morag's singing quietly to herself.

'Vera's a cunt, a freak an a prick, she stinks a piss an shite an sick.'

I stand beside her at the radiator in the playroom. She's got her arms behind her, pulling as hard as she can. The radiator makes squeaking noises. I think she wants it to come loose.

It's dinnertime now; she's been waiting all morning. Vera told her at breakfast, in front of everybody, that she was being transferred to an assessment centre in Glasgow. She said *that's what happens when you misbehave and disrespect the staff at McGregor's.* Morag got up out of her chair and went right up to Vera's face.

'D'ye think it bothers me, ya ugly cunt? Ah'll be glad tae leave this dump.'

Vera sniggered and told the rest of the dining room to ignore her; *this was the type of behaviour that had led to her downfall in the first place.*

Morag slammed the door as she left. That's when she started singing at the top of her voice, 'Vera's a cunt, a freak an a prick, she stinks a piss an shite an sick.'

I think it's because she battered Vera for calling my ma a slut and because she's cheeky to the teachers and she runs away all the time. The last time she got as far as Glasgow Central but a guard stopped her and called the police. She said she gave the police my ma's address in Wallace Street and she was on her way home when they got a message over their walkie-talkies that she was a runaway and had to be returned to McGregor's immediately. Morag said she felt like opening the car door and jumping out when it was moving but they'd locked the doors. Morag's the bravest person I know.

I can't lean against the radiator because she's still pulling at it. I don't want to put my hands near it because Vera might come in and think I'm pulling at it as well.

'Don't take any shite fae any ay them, Puddin, if they start, just get stuck in an kick their cunts in, d'ye hear me?' I nod quietly beside her.

'An don't let that cow pick on ye.' She stops pulling at the radiator and starts kicking it with the back of her heel.

'FAT-ARSED CUNT!' she shouts as loud as she can.

I move over to my locker and pretend that I'm looking for something.

'I think my ma an da might visit wi it bein nearer tae them.'

I close the locker door and stand beside her again.

'Ah'll tell them tae come doon an see ye an ah'll tell them whit that two-faced cunt's really like.'

It's not fair. They probably will go and visit Morag because she's nearer and then they'll forget about me.

Malkey comes into the playroom. He walks over to the window, turns round and leans against the window sill. His hands are in his pockets. He's smiling at Morag.

'My bags are packed an ah'm ready to go ... da da di da-da da da di da ...'

He starts whistling the rest of the tune. Malkey's glad she's leaving because he knows she's not frightened of him. He'd helped Vera get her back for the fight they'd had in the kitchen. They'd both waited till she was sleeping that night, then they went into the bedroom. Malkey held her down while Vera punched her and slapped her. She said she couldn't scream because her face was pushed into the pillow. She said it wasn't the punches that made her cry; it was not being able to breathe. She had bruises round the back of her neck and down her back.

'Away an huv a wank, freak ... It's aw yer good fur.'

Malkey is still whistling but his smile is gone.

'Go an creep around the wee boys an the wee lassies, ya perverted cunt.'

Malkey manages to keep whistling till he is back out of the door.

'If he tries anything funny, go straight tae the main office, don't bother goin tae Vera, d'ye hear me?'

I nod my head again but I think the main office is scarier than Malkey.

Morag finds my hand and squeezes it.

'Ye'd better get tae school or ye'll be late.'

When I get back at quarter to four she's gone.

PART THREE

47

The sun is hot. There is no wind to sway the tops of the corn. I can hear squeals from across the field as the others are being discovered. I've picked a good place this time. The game is hide-and-seek, but it isn't really hiding. The grass is so long that you can flop down anywhere and you're hidden. You aren't really 'found' either. The person who counts comes across people more by accident than by seeking. I'm at the farthest edge of the field.

The long grass rustles beside me. Malkey is edging his way towards me, his elbows pulling him along. Derek's behind him on all fours. Malkey's gold-coloured like the grass, his freckles, his hair, his skin. It takes me a few seconds to spot him. They circle round behind me then lie down in the grass to catch their breaths.

'This is a good spot,' says Derek, sticking his head up as far as he dare.

My chest tightens. My teeth are fixed together. I pull at small clumps of grass beside me to give me something to do but I can tell their position even though my back is to them. Malkey is staring at me. He is still lying down but resting on one elbow, facing towards me.

'He's over at the other end of the field,' says Derek.

I look up. Malkey's grinning straight at me. If I get up he'll either punch me for giving his position away or pull me back down. The grass is tough. It's hard to pull it up. I wind it round my fingers but it won't come out of the ground. I separate it into a smaller bunch and try again.

Malkey sniggers. The only part of my body that's working is my heart, crashing around in my chest.

He's going to get his prick out and ask me to touch it. He always gets his prick out. His eyes are going to close and he's going to make those little moaning sounds. His hand will pull faster and faster and his hips will move with him. The breathing will get quicker and shorter then the white stuff will squirt out and he'll lie back for a minute until his face goes back to its normal colour and his prick gets smaller. Derek starts giggling. I look up.

It's in his hand.

'Touch it, Ailsa . . . gi it a wee rub.'

I add some more grass to the small pile beside me. He wants me to watch him do it but I'm not going to.

'Come on . . . you'll like it,' he says and moves towards me.

I turn my back completely. It's a mistake. He pulls me down and gets himself on top of me. His knee tries to get between my legs. I hold them together as tight as I can.

'I love you.'

He tries to kiss my mouth. I move my head from side to side to avoid his lips and try to push him off. I want my da. I want Morag.

The weight of him pins me to the ground. I can't move underneath him. He reaches for my dress and I know he's trying to get underneath. My arms feel like they're made of cotton wool. I get hold of my pants before he does and hold onto them at the front with both hands. All I can do is keep my legs together, hold on tight to my knickers and move my head out of the way of his wet, breathy mouth.

My knickers are cutting in to me. Derek is looking around to make sure no one's coming. Breathing is hard. There are no sounds except for struggle sounds. The crying won't stay inside. I feel panic, as my hands get weaker.

'Get fuckin aff me . . .'

The sound is lost as it leaves my mouth.

'Let her go, Malkey, she doesn't like it.'

Malkey's eyes are closed. He's rubbing himself against me as he pulls at my hands. His prick is digging into the top of my leg. The crying is stupid. He's unlocking one finger at a time.

I hate this place. I hate Malkey. I hate Derek. I hate the long grass. I hate my ma. I hate my da.

'Let er go, Malkey, it's no funny.'

Derek has raised himself up. Malkey's lips are on my neck; the rubbing doesn't stop.

'Fer fucksake, Malkey . . . get aff er.'

I look at Derek. I want him to help. Derek pushes him hard and knocks him off balance. I'm up. My legs whip through the grass. I don't look back.

48

Maisie tries to scoop up some of the bubbles from the shampoo and squish them between her fingers. I sometimes have to bath the younger ones when Vera or Sarah is busy. Sarah's sewing the gloves onto the pieces of string that go through the arms of the duffle coats. I don't know what Vera's doing.

Maisie's easy to bath. The boys are all bony and their shoulder blades stick out of their backs. They don't like you scrubbing at their knees for the scabs and the bruises. Maisie's a little fat thing. Pudgy fat. Squidgy fat. The fat you'd like to sink your teeth into or nip really hard. She's got these massive long eyelashes that make her look really cute.

Everybody likes Maisie. She's always getting cuddles or giving them. Even the boys cuddle her and sit her on their knees to read her stories. Vera goes on like she's her daughter or something, picking the nicest clothes for her at the Drapery. Holding her hand to walk with her to church. Maisie's allowed to sit in Vera's sitting room until bedtime and Vera takes her upstairs to tuck her in. Everyone else just gets shouted at from her sitting room or the kitchen when they have to go up.

Some of the other ones cry when you rinse their hair because they don't like the water getting in their eyes but Maisie's good. She holds the flannel across her eyes and tilts her head back.

I start to do it almost as soon as the thought comes into my head. My fingers tighten round her neck while her head's tilted back. I want to see what she looks like when she's frightened. I want her to be frightened. I want to see her face get redder and redder. She tries to move her head forward but I won't let her. She starts to make noises in her throat so I clench my teeth to squeeze harder. Her face is bright red. I'm glad she's frightened. I'm glad she cannot breathe.

Her eyes are staring at me. The big tears are stuck to her lashes. I feel ashamed and loosen my grip.

'Good girl, Maisie, nearly done.'

I carry on washing her, holding one leg up at a time. Her face is crumpled with crying. Her hands rub at her eyes. She's still trying to get her breath properly.

'Did some ay the water go in your eyes, Maisie?'

'Ye were . . . chokin . . . me . . . Ah couldny . . . breathe.'

'Aw sorry, Maisie, ah wis just tryin tae get the dirt aff yer neck, wis it too hard?'

I give her a cuddle.

'Don't cry, Maisie, ye'll be awright. Ye kin stay in the bath and huv a swim if ye like. Ye kin swim fur as long as ye like.'

Maisie's breaths are still not back to normal. She stands up to be lifted out of the bath.

'D'ye want some talcum powder, Maisie?'

I bend down to look in her eyes and wipe the tears from her face.

'Ye kin use as much as you like.'

I wrap the big towel round her and run up to the play-room to get the talcum powder out of my locker. When I get back she's shivering, her hair's dripping onto the towel. I hold the tin in front of her and open the lid. I smell it first then hold it to her nose.

'D'ye want some ay this, Maisie? You'll smell lovely.'

She nods her head. I let her hold the talcum powder

while I make a turban for her hair and rub her down gently with the big towel she was wrapped in.

'You put it on, Maisie. Use as much as you like.'

She shakes it onto her belly and her legs and starts to rub it in. I do her back and under her arms. The under her arms bit makes her giggle. She's still holding the talcum powder when her pyjamas are buttoned up and her dressing gown is on.

'Just keep it, Maisie, ah don't really like it that much.'

49

Things were different that day. I should've worked out that something was wrong. It started when I came home from school at dinnertime. Auntie Sarah gave me a huge slice of jam sponge and just a little bit of the lumpy custard. Vera patted my shoulder when I took my plate through to the kitchen. She gave me a note after dinner for the Drapery: one new school shirt, one new school tie, one new pair of black school shoes. Vera said I had to go straight to the Drapery after school and then to the hairdresser's for a trim.

Going to the Drapery was always good, even if it was just for uniform stuff. This time I'd try and get a pair of shoes like Margaret McKinlay's, the ones with the thick heel and the leather tassels.

Vera shouts me into her sitting room when I get back. She wants to check on the clothes and my hair.

'Have a seat,' she says, and pats the cushion beside her on the settee.

Something's wrong. When you go into Vera's sitting room, you always stand against the wall, even if you aren't getting shouted at. My head is trying to work out what I've done wrong.

'Do you remember, Ailsa, the get-well card you sent to your dad recently?' Her voice is really soft. Her eyes don't look angry.

I nod. She'd left a few out on the kitchen table to choose from. I picked the teddy bear with the stethoscope around its neck. She said my da was going to be in hospital for a little while and she thought a card might cheer him up. I wrote him a letter on the inside and told him about Morag moving to another home and getting my knitting badge at the Brownies.

'He wasn't well for a long time.'

She's making me scared with that soft voice she's using and talking about my da like she is. I want to be outside with the others.

'Your dad was an alcoholic, Ailsa . . .'

I can feel my face burn. I don't know what an alcoholic is but I know by the way she's saying it it's something bad about my da. She takes hold of my hand and squeezes it.

'He died this morning from cirrhosis of the liver . . .'

All I can think of is *died*, as in *dead*? Is she telling me that my da is dead? I won't see my da again? I don't believe her. I take my hand out of hers. She's just getting me back for all the times I've been bad. She's paying me back for Morag pulling her hair. My throat holds the words in tight, *Yer a lyin cunt, yer just sayin it so's ah'll be good . . . yer an' ugly, bastard, lyin cunt.*

'The funeral is on Thursday at the Co-op on West Street in Glasgow. I've booked the minibus and I'll come with you.'

She squeezes my hand again and I know it's true. Tears splash onto my jumper. I push my knuckles hard into my eyes to stop them crying. I don't want to sit here and have her look at me. I wipe my face with the sleeve of my jumper. Vera pulls out a hankie from the cuff of her cardigan and hands it to me. It smells of the perfume she wears. I don't know what to do. I rub at the hard bit of skin you get on your finger from writing. The sobs make it hard to breathe.

'If you think you'll be too upset, Ailsa, you don't need to go.'

I can't get a picture of my da to stay long enough in my head. My mind is like a broken-down film, jumping from one bit to the next. The look he had at the parties when he was listening to you announce what you were going to sing. When he fell asleep in his chair and his face was all slack. The time he visited and had that new scar on his top lip. Vera puts her arm around my shoulder. I get up from the settee and shut the door behind me.

The entrance to the funeral parlour is dark. The stands with the vases of flowers are the only things of real colour to be seen. They are either side of the door leading to the room where the service is to be held.

The coffin sits on a platform at the front of the room. Burgundy velvet curtains take up part of the facing wall. A minister, in a black suit, stands in front of the coffin.

Vera edges into the row behind Morag. She has her head buried in her arms, which are resting against the small ledge for the hymn books. I want to sit beside her but I know Vera won't allow it. The minister begins by saying the Lord's Prayer and everyone else joins in. Morag's crying can be heard above the sound of the voices. I feel embarrassed that she is making so much noise. The room is full. I'm not sure whether the faces around me are familiar or not. I look for my ma but she isn't there. I tap Morag's back when the prayer is finished. She turns round. Her face is swollen, her eyes almost closed. She has huge red blotches across her face and neck. She's wearing a denim skirt and a pale-blue Simon shirt. She leans towards me. I move forward.

'Are ye awright?' she says and touches my arm.

I nod. The tears are automatic. I'm crying because I want my da and because Morag looks so sad and because my ma isn't here and because Vera is.

Vera touches my leg and I know it means I have to sit back in my chair. Morag glares at her then turns to face the front. The minister reads a passage from the Bible. I recognise the shape of Big Isa in the second row from the front. My ma isn't with her.

Everyone stands at the introduction to 'Amazing Grace'. The singing is quiet, almost shy. Morag doesn't get up. She rubs hard at the skin on the edge of her thumb. It reminds me of the journey to the Homes in that big black car, when she picked it so hard it bled.

We stay standing while the minister says a prayer. A humming noise starts while he is speaking. The curtains open. The coffin begins to move slowly. Morag puts her head in her hands and begins to rock, backwards and forwards. She doesn't care about the sounds she's making. Big Isa walks up from the front to stand beside her. Her hair is grey and flat. Her nose and cheeks are covered in dark-purple veins. The hankie in her hand is crushed into a ball. She glances at me as she takes her position beside Morag. A second later she turns round and looks straight at me.

'Ailsa?'

I nod. Big Isa smiles and strokes my cheek with her thumb. Her two front teeth are missing.

'Frankie's wain fur sure,' she says and dabs at her eyes with the hankie.

She looks at Vera and nods a hello. The humming stops. The coffin is gone. The minister holds up one hand and closes his eyes.

'The Lord bless thee and keep thee. The Lord make his face to shine upon thee and give thee peace.'

A murmur of soft 'Amens' ends the service. The organ music plays quietly while people leave.

The minibus is parked right outside the funeral parlour.

Vera waits to let me say goodbye to Morag and Big Isa. People stand together in small huddles, lighting cigarettes, blowing their noses. I check the crowd for the last time. My ma definitely isn't there.

Big Isa steps out onto the pavement. She sticks out her hand towards Vera.

'Pleased tae meet ye,' she says. 'Pity it wisny under better circumstances.'

Vera smiles and shakes her hand. Morag cuddles me hard. I want her to take my hand and run with me as fast as she can like we used to when we were younger.

'Ah'll come an visit ye soon,' she says and cuddles me again.

Big Isa still has a hold of Vera's hand. 'Yer welcome tae come back tae mine fur a wee cup a tea,' she says. Morag nudges her.

'That's very kind,' says Vera, placing both of her hands on my shoulders, 'but we'll have to get this one home.'

50

Derek's on the potatoes this week. I'm on the shoes. I can hear him loading the sink up with the potatoes. It sounds like horses running over ground. He runs the tap to cover them with water and take some of the dirt off. It's a rubbish job. Your hands get sore where the peeler rubs against them, plus you're right out in the shed. The sun disappears early evening and it doesn't take long for the tin roof and the brickwork to cool the place down. He keeps trying to be nice to me ever since the day with Malkey but he can go and fuck himself, when Morag comes to visit he's a dead man.

The shoes are a rubbish job as well. What you have to watch out for with the shoes are the spiders and the beetles. They can either be inside the shoe – so you have to shake it hard before you put your hand inside – or they can be under the shoe rack. You always have to check under the shoe rack if you don't have a pair because nine times out of ten, the missing one will be there.

Morag was good at going underneath for you and getting out any stray slippers or shoes. Some of the boys would do it if they were feeling generous. If no one was around, I'd get the yard brush from the shed and use the handle to scoop out the strays. You had to make sure you didn't touch the bristle end of the brush. That could be full of beetles and spiders as well. The polish smells nice though and the shoes look good when you've finished. I go to get the brush. Derek turns the tap off.

'I'll check under the rack fur ye.'

'Don't bother,' I tell him but he's already up there with his arm sweeping backwards and forwards.

'Got one.'

He pulls out a small black shoe with a strap and side buckle. I think it's Maisie McCreedy's. I take it from him without saying anything.

'Ah'll check fur ye the morra an the next day if ye want.'

'Go an get fucked.'

He heads back down to the shed. Vera had a right go at him yesterday. He was rushing to get the big pot up to the kitchen. He tripped and some of the water and a few potatoes fell out of the pot.

'You clumsy idiot, look at the state of the place.'

He started picking up the potatoes.

'Let's hope your sister's got more sense than you.'

Derek stopped what he was doing and looked at her.

'Whit are ye on aboot? Ma sister won't be comin in here, my auntie won't let her.'

Vera got the mop and pail out of the cupboard for him.

'Your auntie hasn't got much say in the matter, seeing as how she has to go into hospital for a couple of weeks and your mother's stuck in court over that business with your father.'

Derek's face was on fire. I nearly felt sorry for him. He rinsed the whole pot of potatoes out and placed them on the cooker. The floor only took a minute to mop. He kept his head down the whole time.

I didn't know Derek had a sister. He never gets any visitors. He doesn't talk about his family or his sister. If she comes here, he better watch out for Malkey.

51

Shona tried to take my bed. Things had been building for a while, since Morag left. It wasn't only her; it was all of them, and it was little things to start with, like getting pushed to the end of the row of the seats in front of the telly. I'd never sat centre, the older ones always got those seats, but Morag always kept me a place beside her, which was near the centre. Then you'd catch them going into your locker and they'd say, *Ah wis just lookin fur ma comic/cards/ marbles* so I hid my felt pens and my book of 'scraps' in the piano stool, underneath the music books. I took my Cindy doll and her two outfits upstairs and hid them at the back of my clothes drawer in the bedroom.

My bed is beside the window. I like it. I like seeing the edge of the tree move in the wind. Sometimes at night I find a tune in my head that matches the movement. Hymns are the best – *We plough the fields and scatter* ... *When the roll is called up yonder*. Then I test myself, if I can get the whole verse sung in my head without the rhythm of the tree changing it means that something good will happen soon.

'Ah'm havin this bed, ah'm sick ay bein stuck in the corner.'

I knew my voice would sound scared even before I opened my mouth.

'Naw yer no ... get tae fuck.' I grab at my sheets, which she has started to unfold. I know that the more she treats it like her own, spreading the sheet, tucking in corners, the more it will become her bed.

'Whit the fuck d'ye think *you're* gonnay dae?' She laughs and grabs the sheet out of my hand. She has this look, like this is what it's going to be like now so you better get used to it.

She bends over to smooth the sheet. This is it. I've seen Morag do it a hundred times. I grab at her hair with both my hands as tight as I can and get her head down on the bed. The rest of her soon follows. Her nails are clawing at my arms and hands but I can't feel them. I keep hold of her hair with one hand and start punching at her ear and the side of her face as hard as I can with the other. If I ease up for a second I'll be done for, I know that. There is no screaming, only the sound of hard breathing from both of us. She's taking the punches and the hair pulling. I don't know what else to do. She's just waiting for her chance to get her head up. My arms are getting tired. The mattress is too soft to bang her against; it'll have to be the bedpost. I can feel her raising herself up even though I'm using all my strength to keep her down. Both my hands grip her hair and ram her head against the wood. It takes three blows to make her cry.

'Yer no havin ma fuckin bed, awright ...' My voice sounds strong. I am strong. 'Ye try that again, ya cunt, an ah'll fuckin kill ye.'

She shouts at me to stop. I loosen my grip. Some of her hair is still wrapped round my fingers. She rubs at the side of her face. It's all swollen. The corner of her eye is closed over. Her hair is sticking up like Ken Dodd's. I want to laugh but I don't.

She gets up and heads for the door. I stay ready, in case she comes back at me. Her feet move quickly across the landing. I hear the lock on the upstairs bathroom door. It's then the shaking starts but I don't cry.

52

I knew I was going to do it as soon as I sat down at the table. And I just knew she was going to ask me. This is Vera's latest idea, that one child says grace for everyone. She picks people at random to make sure they're listening and sitting quietly at the table.

Fish fingers, chips and peas. I quite like fish fingers. I nearly change my mind. Ryan McCreedy sits opposite me. He has snotter crusts around the bottom of his nose and a bubble of snot that peeps out every time he breathes. I feel sick looking at him; his little ratty eyes, his teeth all squashed to the front of his mouth. Most of the kids in here look like him.

Sarah places the last two servings in front of Derek and Shona then pulls herself into the table. Her chair creaks as she adjusts her weight. She's getting fatter. Her overall creases around her bum and hips. The room goes silent.

'Ailsa, would you like to say grace this evening?'

It isn't really a question. No one has ever said no. Ryan McCreedy closes his eyes and clasps his hands in front of him. I clear my throat. I can smell the vinegar on his chips.

'God's a cunt, his son's a prick an Mary's a hoor. Amen.'

Heads turn, eyes open and stare. Silence. I hear her chair being pushed back to let her up. I tighten my body. Vera pulls me out of my seat by the hair. I twist myself round to face her, even though it tightened her grip on my hair. I kick fuck out of her shin and rip at her hands with my nails. She moves back to get out of my range and lets go of my hair with one hand to crack me across the side of the head. My ear throbs but I quite like it. There's room to grab at her hair. She screams as I manage to get her head down. I can see the pattern on the lino and the blood trickling down her leg and the small hole in the toe of her tights.

Sarah comes at me from behind and starts to unravel my fingers from Vera's hair. I have to get as many kicks in as I can.

Vera's voice is shaky. 'Let go of my hair, young lady, right this minute.'

She's breathing really hard and trying to get her leg out of the way of my foot. Stupid cunt. Malkey grabs my legs.

It's over.

Vera staggers back to her seat. I start to cry, not because I'm scared but because I haven't done enough, I didn't get enough time. The heaviness inside hasn't gone away. It sits in the middle of me and fills my insides. Sarah and Malkey carry me into the playroom. Vera limps behind them. The punching and the poking and the slaps are sore but not as sore as I thought they'd be.

'Think you can attack a member of staff . . . an adult in this establishment?'

She is still out of breath.

'Using foul and disgusting language you've brought from the gutter? You're for the same place as your sister, young lady.'

53

Mr Shaugnessy is writing out parts for the recorder group. He passes me a clean sheet of manuscript paper and a fine-tipped, black felt pen. I make some room at his desk.

'You can copy out the descant part, Ailsa, and maybe the tenor if you've got time.'

I begin by counting the number of bars I'll need and putting in the right amount of bar lines. There is no noise except for the slide of our hands every few seconds across the page.

'Would you still like me, Mr Shaugnessy, if ah didny play the piano?'

Mr Shaugnessy stops writing and waits for a few seconds before he speaks.

'Your taking piano lessons, Ailsa, has given me the chance to get to know you and I'm ever so glad I've been given that chance.'

I look up from the page of notes. Mr Shaugnessy looks sad.

'I like you because you're a good person, Ailsa, and you work hard and even though you are going through a difficult time in your life you are able to find beauty in music. I think your gift will help you more than you realise.'

'Ah'm no chuckin the piano, Mr Shaugnessy, ah just wondered.' I carry on with the notes on the page.

Mr Shaugnessy thinks I'm good but I don't feel like I'm good. I feel good sometimes for a little while, like when I help somebody or lend them my crayons, but then I go back to feeling like I'm bad inside and that's the feeling I have most of the time.

'If you say sorry to God, Mr Shaugnessy, for doing something bad but you don't really mean it, does God know?'

'God knows everything, Ailsa, and he sees everything. I think he would be very disappointed if any of his children did not truly regret doing a bad thing.'

'But what if the person deserved the bad thing because they always pick on other people?'

'God will have seen the bad they do, Ailsa, and punish them in his own time. Now he'll be sad because he has to punish two people. He tells us in Matthew 5, verse 39 "whosoever shall smite thee on thy right cheek, turn to him the other also". If we do the same as them, Ailsa, we are not showing them God's way.'

'I don't think you should wait for God to get them, Mr Shaugnessy, I think if you get the chance you should take it and watch the look on their faces. My da says don't let any a these *mmmhs* take the *mmmh* oot ay ye.' I don't say the bad words, I make the noise instead.

Mr Shaugnessy smiles and quietly carries on writing out the notes.

'If you pray to God about it, Ailsa, I'm sure he would help.'

I've done three bars so far and the stems are nice and straight.

'I've asked God for loads of things, Mr Shaugnessy, but he never listens. I've asked for my ma and da to come back, for Morag to come back, for Malkey to leave, for more pocket money, for new toys, to be able to stay up late, to be good at sums, to be good at fighting . . .'

Mr Shaugnessy puts down his pen and empties the jar holding the pens, scissors and pencils onto his desk.

'Pass me the beaters from the glockenspiels and the xylophones, Ailsa.'

I collect about eight or nine altogether. Mr Shaugnessy starts taking the rubber and felt heads off the top of them. He puts as many as he can into the glass jar.

'Is it full, Ailsa?'

I nod. He won't be able to fit anymore in. He takes out a box of drawing pins from his desk drawer and pours them into the jar. He shakes it to make sure they fill up the gaps left by the beater heads.

'Is it full now, Ailsa?'

I check the sides and back. It's definitely full. He takes the Tupperware of sugar out of his brown leather bag and pours the sugar into the jar. It fills up the tiny spaces left by the drawing pins. There is absolutely no space whatsoever left in the jar.

I smile at Mr Shaugnessy. I know he has done something clever but I don't know what.

'The jar is your life, Ailsa. The beater heads are the important things in your life like your family, your health and your faith. The drawing pins represent your schooling, your talents, your friends and your interests. The sugar is everything else; pocket money, sweets, clothes, toys, television etc. What would have happened if I'd poured the sugar in first?'

It doesn't take me long to work it out.

'There'd be no room for the family or the health or the faith or the other things like friends and piano and stuff.'

'That's right, Ailsa. God loves you and listens to you because he's taking care of the most important things in your life. You're in very good health as far as I can see and even though you're not with your family at the moment, Ailsa, they love you very much and miss you as much as you miss them. God will hear you, Ailsa, when you say you're sorry and truly mean it and he'll be happy that one of his children has been guided along the right path.'

I still don't feel sorry for Vera. She's all talk about me being for the same place as Morag, she just takes it out on you in other ways; gives you extra jobs to do and doesn't let you stay up late at the weekends and hands round sweets but lets everybody else pick what they want first. I wish I was for the same place as Morag.

I definitely don't feel sorry for Malkey but I am sorry about Maisie.

'Now then,' says Mr Shaugnessy looking at the jar. 'I should have thought this through a bit more carefully.'

He takes a newspaper out of his music bag and spreads it across the table. I pick out the heads of the beaters, rub them on the sleeve of my jumper, blow on them to get rid of the sugar and attach them back to their sticks. Mr Shaugnessy's fingers are too big to pick out the drawing pins quickly. By the time I'm finished he's only made a little pile. I help him get the rest back into the box. The leftover sugar gets folded into the newspaper and put into the bin. We walk down to the toilets at the back of the stage and wash our hands.

I finish the descant parts then it's time to go home.

54

Mr Shaugnessy says he'll send me a card from Ullapool. He's gone on holiday for two weeks with his wife and grandchildren, Gordon and Fiona. He was telling me how his granddaughter wrote this brilliant poem about a daffodil and described its feelings about being plucked out of the ground to die a slow, miserable death.

It sounds like a stupid poem to me. It sounds like she's one of those lassies you can batter dead easy because they don't know how to fight. She sounds like she wears a hair-band and she's got big teeth. I bet she's ginger and she's got big legs and her eyebrows are really fair.

Another man comes to play the organ on Sunday. He's coming next week as well. I asked him. He's younger than Mr Shaugnessy but he's still got grey hair. It's boring when you can't go up to the music room. You can't even get into the hall because the whole building's locked up except on Saturday mornings when they show a film.

I decide to make Mr Shaugnessy a book about my holidays with words and pictures of what I do every day. I take enough blank pages out of one of my old jotters and Sellotape them together into a new book. On the front of the book I write *my holidays* and draw a picture of me with notes and treble clefs coming out of my head.

At the start of every page I write *practise the piano* and I leave a space to write in the amount of time. Sometimes I write *twenty minutes* and other times I write *fifty-five minutes*. I mostly write *fifty-five minutes*. I draw some more notes and treble clefs around the numbers.

On different days I draw pictures of the park, of the pond, of the swimming pool, of the river, of the film show, of the church and of the telly. I write down what I have for dinner and tea. Ryan lets me borrow his felt pens and I colour it in really nicely. The best day is Wednesday of the second week. I practise for fifty-five minutes. I go to the swimming baths and swim three lengths of the pool. I have pie, chips and beans for my dinner, and then I go on the boats on the pond. I have fish and chips for my tea and a piece of shortbread then I watch telly until ten o'clock.

I finish my book on the second day of my holidays. I put it in my locker to keep it safe. Mr Shaugnessy's postcard from Ullapool arrives on the Monday of the second week. Ullapool looks nice.

55

This is the first time he hasn't smiled or clapped his hands after I've played.

'How much practice did you do this week, Ailsa?'

I know he's disappointed. You can hear it in his voice. I keep my head down so he won't see my eyes beginning to water.

'You know, Ailsa, 1 per cent of success is down to talent; the other 99 per cent is hard work. You've been blessed with this God-given talent but you still need to work very hard.'

The room is quiet.

'I was just telling my wife this morning about the amazing progress you've made over the last ten months.'

I sniff back the snotters that are building up behind my nose and control the big, sad breaths that are trying to get out.

'Are you getting peace to practise, Ailsa? The other children aren't pestering you, are they?'

I still can't speak. The ache in my throat won't let me. The first of the tears splashes onto my hand. I wipe it away with the other hand, sniff back the snotters and check my nose is dry.

'Aren't you enjoying the piano anymore, Ailsa?'

I nod my head quietly but I don't want to look up. I wipe at my eyes again and breathe through my mouth. Mr Shaugnessy squeezes my shoulder and pats my arm.

'Don't get upset, Ailsa – trees haven't withered, the sun hasn't fallen from the sky.'

I don't want him to be nice. It makes me feel worse. I'm angry with myself for letting him down. The sounds escape from my throat. I cannot stop the sobs and the big breaths. I want to go back to last week and practise for an hour every day and not go to the park or watch the telly or colour in books. I want another chance to do better so that Mr Shaugnessy won't be disappointed with me. He gives me the hankie from his pocket and squeezes my shoulder again.

'Let's have a look at the tricky thirds on the second page.'

I give my eyes another wipe of the hankie and take a big breath. It catches in my throat and makes me want to cry again. I put my right hand in position on the keys.

'The trick is to practise very slowly, Ailsa. Then once you've mastered them slowly you can build up the speed.'

I concentrate on making sure both notes go down at exactly the same time until I get to the end of the phrase.

'That's more like it, now, one more time for luck.'

I do even better the second time.

'Excellent stuff, Ailsa, well done.'

He's overdoing the praise to make me feel better. It makes me want to cry again. I promise myself that next week's lesson will be perfect. I'll practise like mad and make him happy again.

'Let's leave last week's instructions the same for this week and see how you get on.'

He pats the top of my head as he gets up to go to his desk. I close the piano books and hold them in a neat pile across my chest.

'Stay for a cuppa, Ailsa, and some chocolate digestives.'

Every time he speaks to me I want to cry.

'If you sort the instrument cases into neat piles over in the corner, the tea'll be ready by the time you've finished.'

He collects together his little plastic bag with the teabags, his medicine bottle full of milk and the Tupperware with the sugar.

'Shan't be long.'

His footsteps clatter on the stairs. I think about what he'll say to his wife when he gets home. *She's no good, Margaret, a waste of time.* The tears come back. My head feels hot.

56

I have the afternoon off school. Mr Shaugnessy is picking me up at one o'clock. When he first told me that he'd entered me for the Greenock Festival, I was pleased. I know he wants me to do well by the way he picks over every bar. There are pencil marks all over the music. Beethoven's minuet in G. He'll say, *They're not only interested in the correct notes, Ailsa, they want an expressive performance.*

Vera is sick of it, so are most of the other kids in the house. When I play it they thump at a bunch of low keys on the piano and moan along to it. Some of them stamp out a dance behind me. Every time Vera passes the playroom she shuts the door.

I'm getting a bit bored of it myself. Sometimes I speed it up as fast as my fingers will go. Other times I play it as staccato as possible. I even keep the pedal on throughout the whole piece until I can't stand the mushed-up sounds anymore. I've even stuck cotton wool in my ears to see what it would be like to be Beethoven. It's hard. You can't hear the tune or how soft or loud you're playing or if you are hitting a wrong note or if you are keeping in time. Mr Shaugnessy said it was a wonder that Beethoven loved music as much as he did because his father used to beat him and drag him out of bed in the middle of the night to play for his friends. They'd all be drunk and even though he was tired he'd have to play tunes on his violin to entertain them. I play it one more time, as good as I can, just in case he's listening.

'He's here,' shouts Vera. I put the lid down on the piano and pull up my socks.

Mr Shaugnessy is standing at the front door. He takes his hat off, smiles and makes his eyes go big.

'All set?' he asks.

I nod, putting my arm through the sleeve of my school blazer.

Vera gives him one of her smiles and tightens the knot on my tie. She spins me round to face him.

'Good luck,' she says, giving him a small wave. The door closes behind us.

Mr Shaugnessy is putting on his gloves as we walk to his car.

'Music?' He looks worried. I wave the sheet music gently in front of him. He smiles and looks relieved.

'It's now or never,' he says, holding the passenger door open for me.

The hall is big with lots of empty chairs. Coats are placed over the backs of some of them. Old women sit on their own or in pairs near the front of the room. A high stage runs almost the full length of the front of the hall. The piano is in the centre. An empty music stand is placed off to the side. A long table sits at the back of the room for the judges. Mr Shaugnessy says there will be three of them and after each performance they will write down their comments. He says under no circumstances am I to start playing until the bell rings to say they are ready.

We stop about six rows from the front and sit on the outside seats. Mr Shaugnessy looks at the programme. Other children stand with adults, some are in school uniform, and others wear hairbands and nice clothes. They are all holding onto their sheets of music. Mr Shaugnessy nudges me and points to the open programme.

My name. Ailsa Dunn. I am fourth out of a group of five. He smiles and pats my arm. People start taking their seats. The three judges take their seats at the back of the room.

A girl with bushy red hair and a navy-blue hairband is the first to play. She walks up the steps, across the stage and sits herself at the piano. She seems to take ages to get herself organised, pulling the stool forward, putting her music on the stand and fixing it in place with the metal pins. The room goes quiet. The girl waits with her hands in position on the piano. Her cheeks are bright red. I feel nervous for her. The bell rings once and she begins to play. Her shoulders start moving and swaying. I want to laugh but then I think, maybe this is what I'm supposed to do. I look at Mr Shaugnessy but he is listening really hard. It sounds good. She doesn't make any mistakes, her thirds are together and you can hear the dynamics throughout. Mr Shaugnessy claps for ages when she's finished. She bows really nicely and smiles at the audience. Her teeth are yellow.

A small boy is next. He plays the piece a lot slower than it is meant to go and then he gets faster and faster. I look at Mr Shaugnessy. He is rubbing his chin. One more girl, then me. I think about getting to the stage. I think about the music falling off the stand. I think about the people looking at my shoes. I want to be back in the music room, playing for Mr Shaugnessy.

The girl before me wears a dark-red pinafore dress and a white blouse with frilly collars. Her hair is in pigtails. They all look different to me, better, shinier.

Mr Shaugnessy tilts himself to the side and whispers into my ear, 'Chopin hated performing, Ailsa. He always got terribly nervous before playing but he produced the most beautiful sounds imaginable and you're going to do the same, don't you worry.'

The girl with the pigtails is walking off the stage. Mr Shaugnessy gets up to let me out.

'Good luck, Ailsa, enjoy it and don't forget to bow nicely at the end.'

We'd practised the bow in the music room. It seemed easy then. You would think there was nothing to get wrong about bowing but there was. It wasn't to be rushed; you had to lower your body far enough down so that it was a definite bow and not just a nod of the head. Your hands had to be by your side or clasped at the front and you didn't pull the sides of your skirt out. *It's important, Ailsa . . . you're thanking the audience for the courtesy of listening well.* It seems an awful lot to remember.

The walk to the stage takes forever and the piano stool surprises me by being heavier than it looks. The music sits properly on the stand, it doesn't bend or flutter. I pull up my socks and look out into the audience for Mr Shaugnessy. My blazer is folded in his lap. He sticks both thumbs up at me and smiles. I listen hard for the bell. Morag would laugh if she could see me. She'd laugh at me sitting on a stage. She'd laugh at me waiting for the bell and she'd laugh at my bow at the end.

The judges are still writing. The room stays quiet except for the odd cough or someone shifting in their chair. I look at the pencil markings on the page. The crescendo in bar six, the rests circled, the slight rit at the end. The bell rings and the room is silent. My fingers find the keys and begin to play.

The first two bars are about finding the right sound, feeling the weight of the keys and adjusting my touch. I forget about the audience. The melody doesn't sound tired and boring. It is beautiful.

Before I know it, the performance is over. The audience clap loudly. Mr Shaugnessy is sitting forward in his chair, his hands raised, smiling and clapping. I bow till I can see the tops of my kneecaps, hands in front of me, holding the music.

The adjudicator is thin and wears glasses. He shifts from side to side as he speaks and talks about being overwhelmed by the talent of the performers and the importance of young players having the opportunity to perform. The adjudicator then goes through each of the performances. Mr Shaugnessy has his pen and diary out. He writes as quickly as the man speaks: *Ailsa's level of musicality is extremely impressive. She has a real sense of what the music is about and expresses this marvellously to her audience. A flawless performance.* I win first prize. The girl with the bushy red hair comes second.

'Are you sure you don't want me to drop you off at the cottage?' Mr Shaugnessy asks as he pulls up outside the main gate.

'This is fine,' I tell him and open the door of his car.

He squeezes my hand. 'Well done, Ailsa, I'm really proud.'

I want to go over everything in my head before I get back to the cottage. I want to remember the hall, the sound the piano made, and the judge's comments. Mr Shaugnessy toots the horn as he drives off. I wave.

The certificate is in a big brown envelope. I slide it out, holding the edge so it doesn't get marked. My name curls and flicks across the centre. It is beautiful.

57

Malkey's leaving. He's going to join the Army and Vera's made a special tea. She places a small present in front of him. The pale-yellow wrapping paper has gold dots all over it and I wonder whether she picked the 'freckle' paper on purpose or if she just liked it.

Malkey opens the card first. It's got a picture of a black cat smiling on the front and the words GOOD LUCK across the top. He puts it down on the table and starts on the present. You can tell it's a watch before he even opens it.

'Thanks very much, Auntie Vera.' He takes it out of the box and puts it on his wrist.

'Let's have a look then, Malcolm,' says Vera, leaning forward in her seat. Malkey holds up his arm with the watch facing her.

'You'll need a good watch, Malcom, for all your travels and adventures. We all wish you lots of luck and safe journeys.' She starts to clap and the others join in. Malkey scrumples up the wrapping paper and puts the lid down on the empty box.

I'm glad he's leaving. I hope the other soldiers kick his cunt in. I hope he gets stabbed with a bayonet and shot through the heart. The doorbell rings just as Vera finishes clapping. Sarah starts slicing a big cake she's placed in front of Malkey. Vera goes to answer the door.

'Hold your plates out,' says Sarah. 'It'll make it easier.'

She's balancing the wedge of cake between her fingers and the flat side of the knife. My slice is good, not too thin. Vera opens the door.

'Ailsa, come here.' Vera's lost her smiley face. She closes the dining-room door behind me and opens the front door. Morag is standing on the top step.

'Awright, Puddin?' she smiles.

Morag looks different. She's taller and wearing make-up. She's got on some red Oxford bags and a white Simon shirt. Her hair's different as well – a feather cut that goes down to her shoulders. I feel shy. I don't know what to say to her. Vera's the first to speak.

'Her social worker is coming back in an hour to pick her up so I've told her you can go for a walk down the park but you'll have to be back by six-thirty.'

I run down to the back and get my shoes and coat on. Vera keeps her at the door.

'Six-thirty, mind, or there'll be trouble.' Vera's got her voice on and her finger out.

'Do we look fuckin stupid, eh?' Morag laughs at her. 'We heard ye the first time.'

Vera slams the front door and Morag sticks her two fingers up at it.

'Moanin-faced bastard,' says Morag, and gets a packet of fags out of her pocket. She takes one out and lights it up. I look around, there's no one there.

'Ye better no smoke Morag, ye'll get inty trouble.'

Morag throws the matchstick away and puts the box back in her pocket.

'They canny touch me doon here, ah'm allowed tae smoke at Thornhill so they kin go an get fucked.'

'Malkey's leavin. He's joinin the Army. Vera's just made im a special tea an bought im a shitey watch.'

Morag flicks her ash on the path. 'Aboot fuckin time,' she says, blowing the smoke out of her mouth. 'Pervy cunt. He husny been up tae his old tricks, has he? Comin inty yer room an that?'

I don't tell her about the cornfield. She'll go mad and it'll just make everything worse and it was nearly a year ago and he hasn't done anything as bad since.

'Naw, Morag, ah just keep oot the cunt's way an ah've shifted ma bed tae beside the windy.'

Morag passes me a bag with some sweeties and chocolates. 'Wire in, Puddin – ah got them fur you.'

I open the Bounty first and offer her a bit but she doesn't want any.

'Yer hair's nice, Morag, an yer troosers are brilliant.'

Morag smiles and flicks the rest of her fag into a bush.

'Ye kin buy yer ain gear at Thornhill, they gie ye an allowance an one ay the workers goes wi ye tae make sure ye buy claes wi the money.' I wish we could buy our own clothes. I'd buy the same stuff as Morag.

'How's the piano, Puddin? Ma social worker says yer doin really well – yer goin tae an academy or somethin?'

I'm surprised she knows so much about me.

'Mr Shaugnessy thinks ah'm good enough tae get inty the Royal Scottish Academy in Glasgow, at the junior school on Saturdays, but ah don't think I am. Ah'm goin fur an audition in a coupla weeks.'

'He widny put ye in fur it, Puddin, if he didny think ye were good enough.' I tell her about the Greenock Festival last year and the big certificate. Morag unwraps a Juicy Fruit and puts it in her mouth.

'There ye go then, Puddin, ye've as good a chance as any.'

We get to the park and sit on the flat bit of the chute. Morag wipes it with her hand before she sits down.

'Is ma ma got a hoose yet, Morag? Is she comin doon tae visit?'

Morag straightens out the bottoms of her trousers so they lie nice against her shoes. 'She's livin wi somebody else noo, Puddin, a right fuckin nutcase. Ma social worker says there's nay chance a gettin back hame while she's wi im. He drinks worse than ma da.'

'But dis she come an visit you Morag?'

She spits her chewing gum on the ground and unwraps another one.

'Dis she fuck. They let me go an visit er a few months ago – two buses an a big long walk. The cunt tapped ma bus fare aff me an bought Callies an fags. She kin go an get fucked, ah'm no botherin ma arse wi er. It took me two hours tae walk it back tae Thornhill.'

'If ye tell er aboot the prize, Morag, an the Academy she might come doon.'

Morag lights up another fag and moves over to the swings. 'She's no interested, Puddin, yer better aff stickin in at the school an the music.'

I think my ma would come down if she heard about the prize and the Academy. The church bell strikes six thirty. We get up off the swings and climb back up the hill.

58

Mr Shaugnessy stops at the steps of the building and looks at the entrance. The words *Royal Scottish Academy of Music and Drama* are carved into the stone. He smiles at me then looks for a bit longer. He doesn't seem to realise that people have to swerve around him to get by. He smiles and pulls his gloves tighter around his fingers. I hope I don't disappoint him.

We're given directions to the room at the end of the corridor on the second floor. The music book is making my hands sweat. My fingers are tight. I lay the book down in the space between us and stretch them wide. Mr Shaugnessy smiles at a woman in a red coat. He takes his gloves off and sticks them in his pocket.

I think about our walk from the train station to the Academy – looking hard to see if I could see someone I knew, getting annoyed with myself when I couldn't make up my mind which side of the street to look at.

'Scales at a steady pace, Ailsa, don't rush them.'

I nod and open my book at the right page.

'Remember the change of fingering in bar five.'

I nod again and play the notes against my leg. The door opens and a tall skinny boy comes out holding a flute and some sheet music. The woman in the red coat stands up and walks towards him. He lets out a big sigh. She pushes his hair out of his eyes. Mr Shaugnessy nudges me and winks. I don't want to let him down.

'Ailsa Dunn?'

Mr Shaugnessy gets up with me.

'Show them what you can do, Ailsa.'

He pats me on the back and stays standing until I get to the door. I shut it behind me and walk over to the piano. I put my music on the stand and pull the stool nearer to the piano.

The man who shouted my name and a woman with white hair sit at a desk to the side of the piano.

'So,' he says, reading from a sheet of paper in front of him. 'You've been playing the piano for about two years ... distinction at grade four ... First in your class at the Greenock Festival ...'

He looks up from the page and smiles.

'You must spend a lot of time practising?'

I nod and smile back at him. My teeth feel too big for my mouth. The woman with the white hair doesn't say anything.

'What other things do you like to do in your spare time?'

I don't know what to say. Mr Shaugnessy said they would maybe ask some questions about Chopin or the meaning of the musical terms on the page. Chopin: 1810–1849, born in Poland, lived in Paris.

'I like watchin the telly.' He smiles. 'I like the Girl Guides.' The woman with the white hair smiles. 'I like readin an drawin and makin pictures wi ma Spirograph.'

He puts the paper down on the desk.

'So you like lots of "arty" activities, Ailsa?'

I nod and smile.

'Would you say you've got an artistic temperament?'

I nod again, twice as hard.

They both smile and sit back in their chairs. I think they like me.

'What are you going to play for us, Ailsa?'

I tell them Chopin's Nocturne in E flat and the man says, 'When you're ready.'

The keys feel beautiful under my fingers. The sounds I want to make are easy on a piano like this and I don't have to strain to keep the left-hand chords quiet to balance with the melody; it sings above my head and fills the room. From the start of the piece I know I'm working towards the con forza passage with the stretto octaves. I know it has to come out of the blue so they can feel the drama of it. The bar before the con forza is clever. It's like a cat pretending to sleep while a mouse peeps out of its hole and just when it thinks it is safe and comes out, the cat comes to life and the chase begins. The long trill at the end ripples evenly to the final *ppp* E flat chords.

The scales afterwards are easy. I play them faster than I should but I don't make any mistakes. I hope Mr Shaugnessy can't hear from where he is sitting.

'Thank you, Ailsa,' says the man, smiling.

The woman is writing on a piece of paper.

'We'll be in touch with you very soon.'

I close my book and push the stool with the back of my legs. I make sure my skirt is pulled down properly at the back. I smile the best I can. I don't know what else to do to let them know I am good and they should pick me. I could tell them about Chopin and how his sister took his heart back to Poland when he died and how nervous he got when he gave a concert.

Both of them have their heads down and are still busy writing. I close the door quietly behind me. Mr Shaugnessy has his hands clasped in front of him, his head is bent. He gets up when he hears the door click behind me. His face is a question. I do the big sigh like the boy before me did.

'How did it go, Ailsa? No mistakes?'

'I played the scales a bit faster, Mr Shaugnessy.' He

looks worried. 'But it was OK, I got them all right.' He takes my music from me as we walk to the stairs.

'Ma fingers wouldny slow down, Mr Shaugnessy, ah kept tryin tae get them tae go slower but as soon as he said "G minor harmonic" they just went mad.'

Mr Shaugnessy smiles. 'What other scales did they ask for?'

I count them off with my fingers: F major contrary motion, two octaves, C minor melodic, four octaves and C sharp chromatic, both hands, two octaves.

'And the Chopin?'

'I didn't go too fast with that, Mr Shaugnessy, I think they liked it. The man wrote something on a bit of paper when I finished playin an showed it to the woman.'

Mr Shaugnessy squeezes my shoulder. 'Did they say when they'd let you know?'

I try to remember what the man said. My feet sound really loud on the stone steps. 'Ah think they said ah would hear quite soon.'

Mr Shaugnessy puts his fist up into the air and smiles. 'It's looking good, Ailsa.'

He opens one of the double doors out into the street. 'Well now,' he says, buttoning up his coat, 'at the very least we ought to be treating you to a nice cup of tea and a slice of cake, eh? What do you think, Ailsa?'

He stops and checks his watch then looks around him. The street is busy. The others'll be jealous when I tell them about the café. I'll tell them I got loads of stuff and they'll be even more jealous.

We turn onto the main street. Mr Shaugnessy points diagonally across the road to an orange-and-white sign that says THE LITE BITE.

The best cakes are snowballs that are made with sponge,

not the chocolate mallow ones, but if they don't have them, then I'm going to have gingerbread with icing on top or a doughnut with icing and Mr Shaugnessy might let me get Irn-Bru instead of tea but if they haven't got Irn-Bru then tea'll be OK as well. I walk ahead of him to get to the crossing.

59

The service is finished and Mr Shaugnessy lets me carry his music out to the car. He waves to the minister and opens the door to the back seat of his car. I hand him the music.

'Next week, Ailsa,' he says. 'You're sure to hear from them next week.' He places the music on the back seat.

I can't speak. I know he expects a smile but I can't.

'Don't you worry about it, Ailsa, I've got a really good feeling about this.'

The tears sit at the front of my eyes, getting bigger by the second. I try to blink them back but they won't move.

He stops and looks at me.

'What's wrong?' he asks, putting his hand on my shoulder.

I put my head down and swallow hard. The tears splash onto my shoes. The black leather under the tear is darker than the rest of the shoe.

Mr Shaugnessy crouches down so that he can see my face.

'It's alright, Ailsa,' he says, trying to get me to look at him. 'Just because you haven't heard yet doesn't mean they don't want you . . . they have dozens of people auditioning, it takes a while. You've done your very best and that's all we can ask of you.'

He gives me a proper cuddle; the smell of his coat and the sound of his voice and the pat of his hand on my back make the sounds escape from inside. I try to get the words out.

'They . . . they said . . . it'd be better here than Glasgow . . . an it wasn't . . . an . . . you're sayin . . . it'll . . . be better at . . . the Academy than here . . . an it won't . . . an . . . ah . . . don't want tae go, Mr . . . Shaugnessy . . . ah . . .'

Mr Shaugnessy takes a hankie out of his pocket and wipes my face. I feel angry at myself. I wish I'd made more mistakes at the audition and hadn't smiled at them so much. Mr Shaugnessy moves me away from him so that I can see his face.

'You've been blessed by God with this talent, Ailsa. You can't waste it.'

I want him to cuddle me again and keep me there forever.

'The teachers at the Academy are going to see how special you are and bring out the absolute best in you.'

I blow my nose on the hankie and try to steady my breathing.

'You're not going to stop coming to the choir, are you?'

I look at him and shake my head.

'You're not going to stop helping me with the cupboards or filing the music or using the room to practise, are you?'

I shake my head again and the tightness in my throat begins to go.

'I'm going to need to listen to your pieces regularly and make sure you're making the right kind of progress, aren't I? I mean, I'm expecting to see just as much of you as I always did, maybe more if you get stuck with something, and I certainly won't manage all those biscuits on my own, Ailsa.'

I smile at the picture I have in my head of Mr Shaugnessy's cheeks bulging and biscuit crumbs sticking to his mouth and chin.

'That's more like it,' he says, getting to his feet. 'Don't

you worry yourself, Ailsa, I'd be lost without my number one girl.'

If I can still see him every day it might not be so bad and if I can still go up to the music room and sit with him, it might not be so bad. If I don't like it then I can tell him and stop going and go back to having Mr Shaugnessy as my teacher.

Mr Shaugnessy toots the horn as his car pulls away from the church. I wave till it turns the corner and disappears.

60

I wait at the end of the path. Mr Shaugnessy said he would meet me at twenty past eight. He thinks we should do a 'dummy run' of the journey to the Academy before the lessons start next week.

He hasn't stopped talking or smiling about the Academy since the letter came. He mentioned it at the Mission Hall two weeks ago and all the old people started clapping. He read out the letter and showed them the award I was given by the supervisor of the Homes, a gold-coloured quaver, on top of a marble stone, on top of a bit of wood, with a little brass plaque. It said *Awarded to Ailsa Dunn for outstanding musical achievement, July 1975.* I thought I'd been called to the main office because I was in trouble. When I saw Mr Shaugnessy there, drinking some tea, I knew it wasn't going to be bad. The supervisor shook my hand and said I was a credit to McGregor's Homes.

On the way back from the Mission Hall, Ina McBride tried to get in the front of the minibus, beside Mr Shaugnessy. She thought because she got to the door first she'd 'bagsed' it. I pushed her out of the way. On the journey back she kept talking to Mr Shaugnessy, telling him how much she liked the choir and how well her violin lessons were going with the new teacher and how she wanted to learn the piano as well. Mr Shaugnessy was being nice to her saying, *Well done, Ina, piano lessons might be a good idea and if you stick at it, you could be as good as Ailsa one day.* That shut her up. I turned round in my seat to get a look at her face but she turned her head to the window.

I can hear his car before I see it. He smiles at me as it pulls up slowly to the grass verge. The clock strikes quarter past eight.

'All set?'

I nod. I feel for the money in my duffle-coat pocket.

'We could drive into the station at Bridge of Weir but I think it's best if we do the whole journey from start to finish eh? What do you think, Ailsa?'

I get in step with him. 'Yeh that's best, Mr Shaugnessy.'

It feels warm, even though it's early and the sun isn't out properly. There's only one other person at the bus stop. He works at the Epileptic Colony. I've seen him walking with some of them when they go to the shop or walk down to the park. They hold onto his arm, even the men. After the 'Morning's, Mr Shaugnessy starts straight away.

'Just taking Ailsa here up to the Royal Scottish Academy of Music and Drama in Glasgow.' He smiles at the man and nods his head. 'She's won a place at their Saturday junior school.'

The man doesn't say anything. He looks tired.

'Hundreds of students audition every year but they only accept . . .'

I keep my eyes on the top of the hill for the first sign of the bus. It's been ages since I've waited at this bus stop. I think about Morag sitting on top of the shelter, swinging her legs. Does she know I got into the Academy? She knew I was doing well on the piano, maybe somebody'll tell her.

I remember the shapes of my ma and da as they walked down the hill, that time they came to visit when we thought they weren't going to come. It would be funny if she came all the way from Glasgow and got off the bus that we were waiting for to take us to get the train to Glasgow. My ma could come on the train with Mr Shaugnessy and me and she could see the Academy and come for a cup of tea . . .

'Are you nervous, Ailsa? The gentleman's asking if you're nervous about starting the Academy.'

I look at him and nod my head. 'A little bit.'

'You'll be fine,' he says, and lights a cigarette. 'Ma granny could play the piano really well, she tried to teach me but ah wis more interested in the football. Ye know whit it's like when yer a wain, ye don't want tae be stuck in the hoose.'

Mr Shaugnessy smiles at him and nods his head. I wonder why he's nodding because he must have liked being in the house and practising when he was young.

'Ah regret it noo right enough. It's a marvellous thing tae be able tae play an instrument.'

'It certainly is that,' Mr Shaugnessy answers him.

The bus seems to pause at the top of the hill and then picks up speed as it makes its way downhill. Mr Shaugnessy's nearest the door when it opens. He climbs on and sits on one of the double seats near the front. The man with the cigarette sits right up at the back.

'Eight twenty-five, Ailsa. You want to be up here just a few minutes before that.'

I nod at him.

'If you leave the house at the same time next week you should be fine.' He gets a packet of sweets out of his pocket and gives me one.

The bus doesn't stop for any more passengers but the driver lets the man out at the junction onto the main street when we get to Bridge of Weir. A small group of people are waiting for it when we get to the train station.

I give Mr Shaugnessy the money from my pocket. The

ticket window is on the left and there's a waiting room on the right. The platform is straight ahead.

'One-and-a-half returns to Glasgow Central please.' The clock on the wall behind the ticket man says eight forty.

'And what time is the next train due?'

'Eight forty-five, sir, and it'll get you into Glasgow at nine twenty-eight.' The ticket man gives Mr Shaugnessy the tickets and his change. Mr Shaugnessy thanks him and we walk onto the platform.

'That's plenty of time for you to get to the Academy, Ailsa. Your first class doesn't start until ten so you'll make it with time to spare.' I nod to let him know I'm listening.

The platform isn't too busy; an old couple sit on the bench, a man stands at the far end reading a newspaper and another man stands near the edge of the platform in front of the old couple.

'Show me where you would wait for the train, Ailsa.' I walk towards the space between the bench and the man with the newspaper. Mr Shaugnessy talks quietly. 'If you're with somebody else, Ailsa, then this would be a good place but when you're on your own next week and the weeks after that, always find a space beside a woman, or a family or some older people. There can be some very strange characters around, Ailsa, who make a beeline for children on their own and their intentions are never good. Always make yourself look like you're with other people.' I walk towards the bench and stand beside the old couple.

'And when you get on the train, Ailsa, sit as near to them as you can.' His face is serious.

'Don't worry, Mr Shaugnessy, if anybody tries tae be funny wi me ah'll go an tell the guard on them.'

'Exactly right, Ailsa, exactly right.' Mr Shaugnessy smiles.

Glasgow Central is really busy. People criss-cross in

front of us and it's hard to keep by Mr Shaugnessy's side. He points to the guards who are talking to people in the station and the long row of ticket windows on the left-hand side.

'All of these people will help you, Ailsa, if you get stuck or somebody is bothering you. Just walk straight up to them, don't be shy. That's what they're there for.'

We walk to the bottom end of the station. People stand in queues waiting for taxis. I like the crowds. It reminds me of the times Morag, Doanal and me used to walk into the city centre.

We cross the street at the lights and walk up Renfield Street.

'Has Ina McBride started piano lessons, Mr Shaugnessy? He stops and stands against the wall to let a woman with a pram pass by.

'Ina McBride? Oh yes, the little girl from the choir. She popped up a few days ago. She's going to start after the summer holidays. Quite a musical girl, doing well on the violin.'

I knew she'd do that, try and get in with Mr Shaugnessy. She's a right show-off with that violin. She carries it all over the place. Robert McGovern calls her 'Ina Corleone' and she goes mad.

It's about the third street on the right. I recognise the church that faces you as you turn into West George Street. At first I thought the church was made out of black bricks but when you look at it closely it's just the dirt from the traffic. We stand on the steps of the Academy and smile at each other.

'We'll go back to the station, Ailsa, and do it one more time, with you showing me the way. Do you think you can do it on your own?'

I nod. 'It's easy, Mr Shaugnessy. Ah bet ah don't even make a mistake. Ah remembered the church fae the last time.'

He smiles and makes a face as if to say well, we'll have to wait and see.

I make sure I walk a couple of steps ahead of him when we leave the station, so he can see that I can do it by myself. I get it right first time. Mr Shaugnessy's happy.

'I think that deserves a nice lunch and some cake at the very least, Ailsa, eh, what do you think?' I smile. He looks at his watch.

'We'll just pop into Biggar's and pick up some theory books and manuscript paper for you on the way, make sure you're all set for next week.'

I get in step with him again.

At the station, on the way back, Mr Shaugnessy shows me how to check the board for platform numbers and times of trains. I spot the sign for platform thirteen and lead the way to the man at the gate. Mr Shaugnessy gives me the tickets to show him. He keeps behind me. I know he's waiting to see what carriage I'll choose and what seats I'll pick. I choose a carriage with a mixture of people and find two seats opposite a woman with a little girl.

When the train starts to move, I take out the theory book and look at the chapter on grade five. The woman opposite must have looked at the title of my book.

'We've just been up to Glasgow to get her ready for starting at the Royal Scottish Academy of Music and Drama next week ...'

61

The room for the aural class is on the third floor. There's already a small group of students waiting outside the door. I try to get my breathing back to normal before I look at anyone in the group. I pretend to look for something in my bag.

Two boys sit on the window sill, while the rest of the group, mostly girls, crowd around them. I watch them for a while. They won't let me catch their eye so I stop trying after a few minutes. The girls are too busy trying to get the attention of the tallest boy, their smiles are big and there's lots of noisy laughing. The smaller boy seems nice enough but he looks a bit like a girl with his long hair tucked behind his ears.

The dumpy girl with the thick black hair and the eyebrows that meet in the middle is making the most noise. 'I'm dreading this lesson; I'm absolutely hopeless with aural tests. It's always my lowest mark in grade exams.'

A thinner girl with a pointed nose joins in. 'It's the theory class I'm dreading. I can never remember where the semitones are supposed to be in the descending melodic minor.'

She fiddles with the green brooch at the neck of her cream blouse. She's wearing American Tan tights under her brown checked skirt. I play the C minor melodic scale in my head; ascending, the semitones come between the second and third and the seventh and eighth. Descending it's between the sixth and fifth and the third and second. I repeat it a few times in my head so I don't forget it.

They don't know that they look weird. If they knew how weird they looked they'd be a lot quieter, they wouldn't draw attention to themselves. They're going on like they're really brilliant or something. The door to the classroom opens and an older man with wavy white hair holds the door open for everyone.

They all rush to get seats together in the two front rows. Eyebrow's got her arm across the seat on her left to save it for the one with the pointy nose. I don't want to sit beside them anyway. Eyebrow thinks I'm bothered but I'm not. I sit in the row behind them. The tall boy with the flute sits in the row beside me. He smiles. He has nice teeth.

'My name is Mr Wallington, a very warm welcome to you all, and happily I have the great pleasure of developing your aural skills over the coming year.' He holds both his hands together in front of him and looks at everyone individually.

'If we could just take a minute to go round the class and introduce ourselves and tell everybody where we are from.' He still has his hands clasped together but he's raised his eyebrows to ask the same question with his face. My body tightens. He nods at the boy with long hair at the end of the front row.

'My name is Callum and I'm from Dunfermline.'

'I'm Jasper and I'm from Edinburgh . . .'

They come from Kelvingrove and Morningside and Bearsden and I can tell by looking at them and the way they speak that those places are nothing like Wallace Street.

'Ma name's Ailsa an ah come fae Glasgow.'

Mr Wallington starts off with chords. He doesn't use a book like Mr Shaugnessy. He doesn't even look at the piano. We have to tell him whether the chord is major, minor, augmented or diminished. We all get them right. He then moves onto inversions of the chords; root position, first inversion and second inversion. Mine is a root position. Thank God.

'Well now, let's see how you do with cadences. Can you put your hands up if you hear a perfect, imperfect, plagal or interrupted cadence?' He starts to play a couple of bars of music.

I don't really like cadences. Interrupted is the only one that is easy. It always sounds like a surprise. Imperfect is supposed to sound unfinished because it ends on the dominant but sometimes it sounds finished to me. A plagal cadence goes from the fourth note to the first and is supposed to sound like 'Amen', but I don't always hear 'Amen' so then I think it must be perfect, the fifth note to the first. I'm not very good at cadences.

Eyebrow's hand shoots up. 'Imperfect.'

Mr Wallington smiles at her. He starts another few bars of music. Some more hands go up at the front. Eyebrow's is amongst them.

'Plagal?'

Mr Wallington nods and smiles at the tall boy. I thought it was plagal but I wasn't sure. We all put our hands up for the next one.

'Interrupted.'

He plays a few more and I only get one right in my head.

'Have a go at the next one, Ailsa.' Mr Wallington smiles at me as he plays the next tune.

Eyebrow turns round to look at me. I can't concentrate. I can't hear what the bass notes do. I can hear the girl sniffing in the front row. I can hear the traffic outside and the footsteps on the landing. I can't hear what kind of cadence it is. My clothes feel tight against my skin. The top of my shirt sticks to the back of my neck and shoulder blades. I stare at the desk to make him think I'm concentrating. He's been waiting a while for my answer. He plays the last two chords again and tells me to listen to the bass notes. I stare at the desk again. He plays only the bass notes and asks me to sing down the steps to the final bass notes. I do it quietly: 'La, la la la la.' The fifth to the first.

'Perfect?'

He smiles. 'Well done, that's absolutely right.'

He thinks I'm a dummy. They all do. I give Eyebrow the dirtiest look I can and she quickly turns back round in her chair.

Mr Wallington gets up from the piano. 'That'll be all for this week but might I suggest you get your hands on a hymn book and get one of your friends or family to play the final cadences of a few hymns to give you a bit of extra practice. Good work. Well done.'

I let the others go out ahead of me. That Eyebrow better watch herself.

62

The room is bare and surprisingly dull considering the size of the window. You could stand on the window sill, stretch your arms and stand on tiptoe and still not reach the top of it. There is an empty glass bookcase against one wall and the baby grand piano sits in the middle of the room. Three music stands huddle in the corner. There are no pictures, no books, no instruments and no colour except for the brown damp stain in the corner of the high ceiling. The sun has either gone or not reached this side of the building yet.

Miss Ross looks up from making notes in a little red diary. She looks out of place in the room, like an exotic bird in a town square full of pigeons.

'Hello,' she says and holds out her hand. 'You must be Ailsa.'

I nod and shake her hand.

'I'm Miss Ross,' she says and smiles.

She has small, narrow teeth. They're really white but they crowd each other and overlap at the front. In her long printed dress and turquoise, dangly earrings she reminds me of the social worker that took us to McGregor's. Her hair is short and curly. She pats the music stool beside her. I take my coat off and place it on the window sill.

'I've had a look at the notes made by my colleagues during your audition, Ailsa. Well done. They were very impressed.'

I hold the music books closer to my chest and smile at her.

'Well, let's hear what you're made of, eh?'

I pass her the books and she begins to flick through the pages.

'Ah've done the Nocturne in E flat, the Mozart Sonata in C and the first two movements of the Sonata in F.'

She flicks through the other books.

'Ah've done some Bach Inventions and some Preludes and Fugues.'

She asks if I've done any Debussy or Ravel or Bartok. I shake my head.

'Your choice, Ailsa, play me something that you feel connected to.'

My head fills up with all the pieces I've ever played. Mr Shaugnessy said if she asked for a piece to do the Nocturne but I'm sick of playing the Nocturne. I take the Mozart from her lap and flick to the Adagio, the second movement of the F major. She nods and smiles and sits back in her chair.

The sounds feel different in this room; they bounce all over the walls and the ceiling, filling up the whole space. The sforzandos are more like fortissimos and the pianos don't seem to get softer than mezzo piano. Mr Shaugnessy would say *a bad workman quarrels with his tools, Ailsa* so I try to adjust as I go along. Apart from the odd slip and the harshness of some of the sounds, it seems to go pretty well.

Miss Ross moves forward in her chair. She is nodding as she speaks.

'Well done, Ailsa, it's a very bright piano and you cottoned onto that very quickly. You're using a bit too much rubato throughout which makes it far too senti-mental, Mozart wouldn't thank you for that.' She flicks the pages backwards and forwards.

'Some of the trills were a bit untidy and your phrasing needs to be much clearer . . . let me show you.' She stands up and I get off the stool to let her sit down.

She moves quite a lot when she plays. My heart sinks. I don't want my shoulders to move like that. I can't concentrate on her phrasing. The swaying is putting me off. Mr Shaugnessy doesn't move around like that.

'Can you hear the difference?' She plays the right hand only. It seems exaggerated. I nod.

'Have another go.'

We swap places and I try to make the breaks where she did. My shoulders stay where they are.

'Much better, Ailsa, and much more disciplined in the tempo.'

I feel like a robot. It doesn't sound right or feel right but she seems to like it more.

While she writes a list of books I have to get for the following week there is a quiet knocking at the door. She shouts without lifting her head, 'Just a minute . . .'

I pick up my coat from the window sill and collect my books from the top of the piano. She hands me the list and smiles. 'And bring a little notebook with you next week so we can keep track of what you're working on. Good work, Ailsa, see you next week.'

A boy steps into the room as soon as I open the door.

'Hello,' says Miss Ross, 'you must be Roger . . .' The door clicks softly behind me.

63

Vera's up to 'high doh'. A big busload of women is getting a tour of our house. They do that sometimes, in the spring and summer months. Vera says the women raise a lot of money in their churches for the Homes so it's the least we can do. The place is immaculate.

They come right inside the house and go up to your bedrooms and they talk about how neat the corners of the bedspreads are and how shiny the linoleum is on the stairs. They point and smile at the rows of school photos on the dining-room wall and the rows of flannels and toothpaste mugs in the bathroom. They look posh with their hand-bags and gloves.

Vera's made us tidy our lockers because she likes to show them everything. Ryan got skelped on the back of his head because he twisted the curtain when she asked him to close the window and he didn't fix it afterwards. I know I'm supposed to smile at them and keep quiet unless they speak to me and be on my best behaviour the whole time that they're in. You're not allowed to be shy either. If they speak to you and you just smile and nod, Vera goes mad when they've gone. *Why didn't you open your mouth? They'll think it's a houseful of imbeciles we're looking after.*

The doorbell rings.

'Good afternoon, ladies, come in, come in.' Vera holds the door open wide and about a dozen of them squeeze into the hallway.

'The rest of your group are going to Cottage 8, I believe?' Vera scans the faces of the women. They nod and smile at her. 'Well between you and me, ladies, I'd say you'd got the better deal.'

Some of them start giggling and some of them put their hands to their mouths and smile at each other. The one at the front hands Vera a big tin of biscuits.

'Just a little treat for the children at teatime.'

Vera's got her thankful face on. 'You are really too kind, ladies. You already do more than enough but it's very much appreciated.' Vera puts the tin on top of the sideboard.

'Shall we start upstairs and work our way down?'

They all follow Vera. Some of the older ones hang onto the banister rail. She starts straight away.

'The children change their bedsheets once a week and make their own beds every morning. We feel it's important for them to learn good housekeeping skills at an early age.'

The women make approving sounds back at Vera. Once they are upstairs, you can only hear the trample of their heavy footsteps. The smell of the polish and floorwax is giving me a headache. After ten minutes they start to come back down-stairs and head for the playroom. Vera always picks Maisie and Derek's lockers to show them. They've got the best toys.

'As you can see, ladies, our children want for nothing, thanks to the generosity of groups like yours.'

Vera leaves the doors of the lockers open so that the rest of the group can have a look inside. They look around at the square of carpet, the shiny floors at the far end of the room and the piano against the wall. They smile at us while we sit at the table beside the window. Ryan pretends he's reading a book. Shona and Maisie are colouring in. Some of the boys start giggling. I look at Vera. She's trying to give them the look but their heads are down. Vera moves across to the piano and opens the lid. My shoulders tighten.

'I'm sure you'll be thrilled to know, ladies, that your

generosity extends far beyond the basic provision these children need. One of our girls has recently won a place at the Royal Scottish Academy of Music and Drama Saturday junior school.' The women turn round to look at us, trying to work out which one it is.

'As a matter of fact, I know Ailsa would like to show her gratitude and play something for you.' Vera gives me the look. 'Your money pays for her fees and travelling expenses and without your generous support, it wouldn't be possible to encourage the talents of the children in our care.'

The women look delighted and I start to feel bad about the thoughts in my head: *How would you like me to walk around your house? How would you like it if I looked in your bedroom and in your cupboards and if there weren't enough smiles from you there'd be trouble?* I sit at the piano and the women move closer. 'Spring', by Grieg, always goes down well. Pretty enough for them to enjoy and in places it sounds more difficult than it actually is. It's hard not to give a mechanical performance. They start clapping and *oohing* and *aahing* at each other when I finish. Vera has her best face on. I smile at them and have the answers ready for their questions. *How old are you, Ailsa? How long have you been playing?* I nod when they say, *You're a very lucky girl, aren't you?* It's the only time I wish I'd never learned the piano.

The church warden comes back to collect them after forty-five minutes to give them a tour of the grounds. Sometimes, if you walk past them when they're on one of their tours, they slip you some sweets or give you ten pence. I don't want to take their sweets or their money but I always do.

64

The café is warm. It's only a few hundred yards from the train station. There's never very many people in at ten past nine on a Saturday morning. It's quiet inside except for the noise from the coffee machine. It spits and splutters throughout the morning. The steam from it snakes its way up to the ceiling tiles then curls back down and spreads itself out until it disappears.

I don't sit at the window, even though there are three tables to choose from. Someone might see me. I sit on the side wall where I can still watch the people going by. I like watching people when they don't know they're being watched. I make up stories in my head about where they've just come from and what they are on their way to do. Last week a woman passed the window and she smiled to herself and started shaking her head. I decided that she had just come from her own house where everyone had been acting strange because even though it was her birthday, no one had said happy birthday. She thought her family had forgotten all about it. She got her bag as normal and put her coat on to nip to the shops. Halfway down the steps of the close, she realised she'd left her purse in the kitchen. When she went back to get it she heard her husband on the phone planning a surprise party for her. That was why she was smiling to herself. It's fun making up stories about the people and it helps pass the time. For days afterwards though, I thought about what had really made her smile.

I wonder if there's someone sitting in a café in Glasgow, watching my ma pass by. They'd like looking at my ma, she'd be wearing her black skirt that my da liked and the white blouse with the pearly buttons. Her hair would be wavy and bouncy and her legs would look nice in her nylons and her black slingback heels. Nobody prettier than my ma passes the window. Some are nearly as pretty but nobody is prettier.

I use the money for train fares to buy food. I have to make the Irn-Bru last a long time so I always ask for a straw. If I get a bacon sandwich then that's the money gone. If I get toast, there's enough left over for a Tunnock's caramel wafer later on. I usually get the toast and the biscuit.

I look at the clock on the wall. Twenty past ten. They'll all be sitting in the classroom now: perfect, imperfect, plagal and interrupted. Eyebrow'll have her hand shooting up every two minutes. Who'll be the worst in the class when I'm not there? Who will she turn and stare at when they don't know the answer? Fuckin swot. I imagine what it would feel like to punch her hard on the back of the head. They say if you have special powers and concentrate hard enough, you can make things happen hundreds of miles away, just from the power of your mind. Uri Geller does it bending spoons. I close my eyes and see the back of her head and her thick, dark, frizzy hair. I pull my arm back as far as it'll go and keep my fist hard and tight. The punch is quick and it doesn't hurt my hand at all. Her hands go to the back of her head and she turns round. Her face is scrunched up and her eyebrow wrinkles across her forehead but there's nobody there. I smile to myself and take a sip of my Irn-Bru.

65

Vera opens the front door as I walk up the path. She stands with her arms folded across her chest.

'Good lesson today?'

I can tell by her face that she knows. She points at her sitting room as I walk up the steps. Mr Burton, the supervisor, is sitting on the small settee, fiddling with his car keys. He doesn't say anything. He gives me a long, tired look while Vera closes the sitting-room door behind her and takes her seat.

'Five weeks you haven't attended, madam. Have you got anything to say for yourself?'

I don't speak. I don't care what they think. Vera's only bothered about looking bad in front of Mr Burton. She doesn't care whether I go or not.

'Believe you me, Mr Burton, to hear her on a Saturday you'd think she'd trekked halfway across the world. *The train was really busy, Auntie Vera, my teacher was really pleased, Auntie Vera . . .*' Her mouth is tight. Her eyes are black pebbles.

Mr Burton sits forward in his seat.

'We pay a lot of money for you to go to the Academy, Ailsa.'

His disappointment shouldn't bother me – I hardly know him – but it does.

'That money could easily be spent on other things, but Mr Shaugnessy's faith in you, and the high opinion of the staff at the Academy, would suggest that it would be money well spent.'

It's only when Vera starts going on about Mr Shaugnessy that the tears come.

'He's going to be so disappointed when he hears about your carry-on. He's never done talking about how talented you are and how proud he is of you.'

I want my ma. I want my da to get Vera by the throat and tell her to pack it in. They start with the questions. *Why haven't you been going? Where have you been going instead? What happened to the expenses money? Who else knew you weren't going?* I answer all their questions and promise them I'll definitely go next week.

Mr Burton nods his head. 'I'm pleased to hear that, Ailsa, because we've already spoken to Miss Ross and asked her to sign your notebook every week so that we can keep an eye on your attendance.'

I nod at him. He gets up to leave. Vera takes the cup and saucer from the table beside him and puts it back on the tray. My voice sounds croaky.

'Mr Burton, will ye no tell Mr Shaugnessy? Ah promise ah won't miss it again.'

They both look at each other. Mr Burton rubs at the corner of his mouth with his finger and looks at Vera again.

'I can only speak for myself, Ailsa, but you're in no position to be asking for favours of anyone right now. You've let us all down really badly and you've got a lot of making up to do.'

Vera picks up the tray and looks straight at me while she talks to Mr Burton.

'Maybe it's about time, Mr Burton, that Mr Shaugnessy found out what his "golden girl" is really like.' Fresh tears sting at my eyes. 'Maybe he should get to see what the rest of us see, an ungrateful, spoilt little madam.'

Mr Burton doesn't say anything but he looks at me for

a long time. I try to make everything about me show him how sorry I am.

'Get yourself straight up to bed, young lady, and you'll stay there till tomorrow morning.'

I hold the door to let Vera out with the tray.

It feels strange, to be in pyjamas, in bed at four o'clock in the afternoon. I think about all the ways I can be good so that Vera won't tell Mr Shaugnessy. I won't talk to the others when they come to bed. I'll do extra jobs to help her. I'll knock on her sitting-room door every night and ask if she wants a cup of tea.

My fingers play the opening bars of Chopin's Prelude in E minor on the bedcovers. It's the saddest tune I know and I want it to make me cry. I deserve it. I am everything Vera says I am but I don't want Mr Shaugnessy to know I'm all those things.

Smells from the oven reach my bedroom. I think it's sausage rolls. It feels like weeks since I had the toast and Irn-Bru in the café this morning. Vera's Scholls flip-flop across the kitchen floor, plates are noisily laid out on the kitchen table for serving. The dining-room chairs scrape across the floor as they take their places at the table. If it's sausage rolls there's probably beans with them and after the sausage roll and beans there'll be some cake or short-bread or rock buns. Sarah will be going round with the teapot while they're all tucking in. I stop thinking about food. I think instead about how I will apologise to Miss Ross and how hard I will practise so that she knows I'm going to be better and even though I can't do half of those ear tests I'm going to listen really hard and get as many as I can and I'm going to ask Mr Shaugnessy if he'll give me extra practice with them.

The theme music for *Dr Who* is playing on the telly.

When I get up tomorrow I'll show Vera how good I can be and she won't tell Mr Shaugnessy about the Academy.

The boiled egg at breakfast is the best boiled egg ever. There's a plateful of toast in the middle of the table. When the egg is finished I put marmalade on the toast instead. Ryan asks why I got sent to bed. I carry on marmalading my toast and don't answer him. Vera doesn't like speaking at the table. When breakfast is over I help Shona clear the table. I'm on drying dishes this week but I help Shona quickly while Derek fills the sink. When the dishes are dried I hang the dishtowel up on the peg.

'Will ah help Maisie get ready fur church, Auntie Vera?'

She's getting the chicken out of the fridge. She plonks it down on the draining board by the sink.

'Make sure she wears her new navy coat and shoes.'

I go upstairs to find her. Maisie looks cute in her vest and pants. She bounces on the edge of her bed while I try to get her socks on.

'Keep still, Maisie, ah canny get yer socks on straight.'

She starts singing 'Jesus Wants Me for a Sunbeam'. The pale-blue dress with the white daisies is getting too tight for her and when I get her to lean forward so that her hair doesn't get caught in the zip, it just makes her back wider. I stand her up and get her to hold her hair up in a bun. The zip goes up eventually. She turns round and the pleats at the front don't hang straight because her belly is sticking out. I put my head against the fatness of her and cuddle her for as long as she'll let me. After a few seconds she wriggles free.

Her new shoes are the hardest. The buckle is really stiff and she won't keep her legs still. It takes ages to get the strap through and the pin into the right hole. I get the brush through her hair a few times before she starts putting her hands up to stop me. Her new coat is the last thing to go on. I make her twirl around a couple of times then stand her in front of the mirror.

I quickly get changed while she admires herself in the mirror. I don't want Vera to go mad because we're not lined up on time. I hold Maisie's hand as we walk down the stairs. Some of the others are already lined up at the front door. Maisie goes to the front of the line and takes Vera's hand. Vera's wearing a pale-blue two-piece and a navy hat with matching gloves, shoes and bag. I could tell her she looks nice but my mouth won't let me.

On the walk to church I don't misbehave, even when Derek starts walking like a German. I keep my eyes on Vera at the front. She'll turn round at any minute to check on everybody and I don't want to be caught doing something I shouldn't. We climb the steps to the entrance of the church and follow the left-hand line, through the door, down our side of the pews. Vera stops to make sure everyone puts their money in the collection box. I can hear Mr Shaugnessy on the organ.

The words tumble out of me. 'You look really nice, Auntie Vera.'

She ignores me and waves at the others behind me to hurry up. When we get to our pews at the front, she rearranges the seating. Ryan and Gary sit on either side of her and Derek is right in front, so she can poke him if he starts misbehaving.

The service is as slow as always. Maisie skips off to Sunday school with the others after the first hymn. She waves at Vera and anyone else who will wave to her. The minister gives the details of the reading and waits a few seconds to let people look it up. Vera finds it in her Bible and follows the words with her fingernail. She keeps her head bowed longer than anyone else, even when they've closed the Bibles and put them on the shelves in front of them. The minister gives the number of the next hymn and tells everyone it's one of his favourites, 'How Great Thou Art'. Mr Shaugnessy plays the introduction and everyone stands up. Vera sings loudly in that wavery voice of hers. She doesn't use the hymn book. She puts her hands behind her back and sings with her head and chin pointed to the ceiling. Vera loves being in church. During the prayers she clasps her hands in front of her and rests them in her lap. Her eyes are tight shut, like she's really praying, and at the end of it she always says a loud 'Amen'. When the minister gives his sermon, she doesn't take her eyes off him, except to scan the row a couple of times, or poke someone in the back, or their knee if she can reach. If she has to lean forward to catch the eye of whoever's misbehaving they're in big trouble. I've been good. I haven't swung my legs or flicked through the pages of the hymn book or nudged the person beside me. Vera's bound to have noticed how good I've been.

The service finishes at last. Mr Shaugnessy plays the music while the people leave quietly. The people in the back rows leave first. Our pews are right at the front on the left-hand side. Vera is at the aisle end of the row. As soon as it comes to our turn to leave, instead of standing in the aisle to make sure we leave quietly like she usually does, Vera walks down to the front of the church and across to the right. My eyes follow her. Maybe she's going to speak to one of the house-parents on the other side. Maybe she's going to look at the flowers in the big vases on either side of the altar. Vera keeps walking. She doesn't stop to speak to anyone. She doesn't stop to look at the flowers. She stands at the side of the organ, waiting for Mr Shaugnessy to stop playing. I can't breathe. My legs won't move forward.

Mr Shaugnessy smiles that big smile of his and leans over in his seat to hear what she has to say. I can't see Vera's face, only the back of her scabby fuckin coat and her thick, bastard legs. She's an out and out cunt and my hate for her burns all over me. Mr Shaugnessy stops smiling and puts his arm across his chest and rests his chin in the other hand. His head makes small nodding movements while he listens to her. I know what she's like. She'll be making it sound a million times worse than it is.

I catch up with the others and hide myself amongst them. Once we get out of the church I get ahead of them. The tears splash onto my chest. I think about the following Saturday. As soon as I get to Glasgow I'll ask people for directions to Wallace Street and then I'll tell my ma what she's like and she'll come back with me, kick Vera's cunt in and then take me back to Glasgow. Then I remember Morag saying she's moved to Springburn. I don't know where Springburn is. But if I ask people they can tell me which bus to get and when I get there I'll just knock on people's doors and maybe I'll knock on hers and she'll answer it and get a big shock and say, *Fucksake, Puddin, whit're ye dain up here?* and I'll tell her and she'll put her coat on and jump on the train with me, kick Vera's cunt right in, then take me back to Springburn.

The tears come harder. My ma's not going to do anything. If she cared, even a little bit, she'd come back.

Mr Shaugnessy won't like me anymore. He won't want to talk to me or have me help him in the music room. Vera's ruined everything and there's nothing I can do to get her back. She won't care if I don't talk to her ever again. She'll make fun of my silence to everyone else. *If madam thinks I'm bothered about her not speaking then she has another think coming.*

Vera comes in after everybody's sat at the dinner table.

She's humming 'How Great Thou Art'. She hangs her coat on the peg behind the door and takes her seat at the top of the table. She speaks to Sarah but it's really to everyone. 'Well now, it looks like madam has some explaining to do to her precious Mr Shaugnessy.'

I look across at her. It starts with a smile then turns into a giggle. I put the fork down and try to swallow the piece of potato in my mouth. Ryan looks and starts giggling as well. Vera stares at me. Her fork is halfway to her mouth. The piece of chicken on the end of her fork drips gravy. I point at her head and laugh even louder. Vera feels her head with her free hand and quickly takes the fancy hat off. Her face twists in annoyance. She puts her fork down and gets out of her seat to place the hat on the sideboard. She catches me making a *how stupid did she look* face at Ryan.

'Get on with your dinner, the pair of you, or you'll find yourselves in bed for the rest of the afternoon.'

I smile as I put the food into my mouth. Ryan puts his head down and doesn't look at me. I make sure I keep smiling throughout the whole meal.

66

Mr Shaugnessy isn't at school the next day. We get music straight after dinner but the assistant head takes the lesson instead. He makes us copy out a chapter from the 'Instruments of the Orchestra' books. At the end of the lesson, I collect in the books and put them back in the cupboard.

'Is Mr Shaugnessy not well, sir?'

Mr Bannatyne looks up from his newspaper. 'None of your business, young lady. Get yourself to your next lesson pronto!'

He isn't up at the music room. I check after school. The main doors are locked and his car isn't outside. I wait on the steps for nearly an hour. Mr Shaugnessy is never absent. Other teachers go off on the sick and the rest of the teachers stand in for them but Mr Shaugnessy has never been absent. Never. He isn't at school for the next four days. I ask different teachers if they know why he isn't at school but they don't give me a proper answer. They say things like *Nowt to do wi nosey folk* and *Mind your own business, lady*, and carry on with whatever they are doing.

I don't want his absence to be because of me. What if he's so disappointed with me he doesn't want to work here anymore? What if he's already handed in a letter of resignation and won't come back? What if he thinks it's a waste of time working here because the children are too ungrateful?

I'm fed up with nobody telling me anything. I walk up to the Headmaster's door and knock on it quickly. His secretary gets up from behind her desk and puts both her hands on my shoulders and turns me away from the door. I tell her why I want to see Mr Bennett and she says, 'You'll not be bothering the Headmaster with your nonsense.'

I shake her hands off my shoulders. 'It's not nonsense, I just want to know where he is.' She pushes me through the double doors into the main hall.

'D'ye know when he's comin back?' The doors start to close slowly in front of me.

She looks flustered. 'I'm sure Mr Shaugnessy's got enough on his plate at the moment, young lady.'

I don't know what she means by 'enough on his plate'. Does that mean he's not well? Has something happened to him? I get pictures of him mangled up in his car or lying in hospital with bandages around his head.

I shout really loud. 'WHIT D'YE MEAN "ENOUGH ON HIS PLATE"?'

I can hear the heavy click of her office door. I go up to the music room at dinnertime just in case he turns up. There's no sign of him.

Mr Shaugnessy isn't at church on Sunday. Another man takes his place at the organ. The minister welcomes everyone to the service, '. . . and let us remember Mr Shaugnessy and his family in our prayers.'

I feel like I'm going to fall, even though I'm sitting down. Why is he saying that? What does it mean? I listen to every single word he says, especially the prayers, but he doesn't mention him again. The service takes forever. Eventually it comes to an end. The church warden holds the bottom door open for the minister. I don't wait for our row to leave. I'm near the end of the aisle. I get up and head for the bottom door.

Vera hisses behind me, 'Where do you think you're going, young lady. Get yourself back here.'

I don't turn round. I push the bottom door open and follow the minister into his office.

'Whit's wrong wi Mr Shaugnessy?'

The minister turns round and leans his right ear towards me.

'Ye said we hud tae remember Mr Shaugnessy an his family in our prayers. Why did ye say that? Is he OK?'

The minister pushes his glasses up to his eyes. 'It's nothing for you to worry about, he . . .'

'Sorry about this, Reverend.' Vera moves me away from him. She's got her 'goodness' face on. 'You need eyes in the back of your head, don't you?' He smiles and shuffles round to his desk. She pokes me hard, in the back, as soon as he's turned round and marches me straight out of the church.

'Think you're a law unto yourself, madam. You'll spend the rest of the day in bed . . . disobeying my instructions.'

I get free of her and walk quickly ahead. I don't get changed for bed. I wait till I hear the cutlery against the plates and I take my shoes off and hold them in my hand. I keep to the edges of the stairs. The creaks always sound loudest in the middle. When I get to the shed I put my shoes back on and head out the door.

The manse sits behind our cottage. It takes a few knocks before anyone answers the door. The minister stands in front of me in a dark-green cardigan and open-necked shirt.

'Ah'm sorry tae bother ye, Mr Forsythe, Auntie Vera sent me over tae see if ye had Mr Shaugnessy's address so we kin post the card tae him an his family?'

The minister frowns for a second, like he's trying to think of it.

'His address, you say . . .' He pats at his trouser and cardigan pockets. After he's felt all of them he stops patting. 'A card's a lovely idea but I'm sure if you hand it in to the main office tomorrow, they'll post it for you.' He puts his hand to the front door like he's going to close it.

'Ah'm gonnay post it first thing in the morning, Mr Forsythe. The office might no post it fur a few days.' He doesn't move from the door.

'It took me ages tae make it, Mr Forsythe.'

He smiles. 'Well I know he lives in Kilmalcolm but I'm not entirely sure where . . .' He moves to the table beside his phone.

Kilmalcolm's only a few miles away. It won't take long to get there.

'Yer service wis really good this mornin, Mr Forsythe. Ye picked good hymns as well.'

He turns round with the address book in his hand. 'I'm sure it's Woodlea Road but I haven't marked it down in the book.' His wife shouts at him from the kitchen. 'Why don't you ask at the main office tomorrow, then post it yourself?'

I nod and smile at him. 'That's a good idea, Mr Forsythe. Thanks very much.'

I cut across the park and get to the small bridge on the windy road that takes you up to the main road. I drop down the other side of the bridge and start walking across the field. My shoes get dirty in the soggy field and my socks are splashed all the way up my leg. Vera's going to go mad when she realises I'm not in my bedroom. I don't care. Fuck her. Ugly cunt. Every squelch is me standing on her guts. Imagining her face is the best. I can see it on the ground before me. I stop, put both feet together and jump as hard as I can. Her face is a splattered mush of purples and reds and jelly eyeballs.

The traffic thunders past on the top road. I follow the direction of it but stay in the field. There's a big clump of trees straight ahead. I can't see what's on the other side.

It only takes about fifteen minutes to reach them. Once I come out the other side I can see at least two more fields before I get to the big house that stands on its own. The second field has cows. I don't like cows. I don't like their pink eyes and slavvery mouths. I don't like their wet nostrils and the way they walk, like they're too heavy for their own legs. I don't like the way they tear at grass, ripping it from the ground and grinding it between their teeth. When I get to the field with the cows, I'll stick to the edges.

What if Mr Shaugnessy's not in? What if nobody's in? I dig my hands deep into my pockets. Maybe his neighbours'll know what's happened to him. The house is further away than it looks. I've been walking for ages and it still seems no nearer.

Mozart's Rondo from the Horn Concerto bounces around in my head. My steps keep time with the music. Mr Shaugnessy played it in class a couple of weeks ago to explain 'rondo' form. It was easy; it went ABACAD and so on. We had to put our hands up every time we heard the return of the A theme. As soon as the music started, he moved his head from side to side in time with the music and conducted it with small movements from his right hand. Somebody at the back started sniggering because he was moving his head like that but he was just enjoying it. Mr Shaugnessy didn't realise but he gave it away every time the A theme came back. The bar before it returned, he'd lean forward and stop all his movements. He stood like a statue, waiting for the hands. He smiled when lots of hands went up and went back to shaking his head in time to the music. Mr Shaugnessy looked really happy. He didn't look like he wasn't well; he just looked normal.

A horn blasts from one of the lorries on the main road. The cows don't look up. I keep close to the fence. If they start coming towards me I can get over it quickly.

All Cows Eat Grass.

When Mr Shaugnessy told me about the ACEG spaces in the bass clef I imagined a cow with each of its four feet in a different space, munching on the notes above the stave. The cow on my stave was black with lots of white, fluffy-shaped patches on its body and it had long curly eyelashes and a swishy tail. These cows are smelly and their legs are covered in mud. The white patches on their brown skin aren't white, they're yellowy-grey and the hair on their bodies isn't smooth and clean, it's matted and dingy. These cows are ugly, their bones stick out at their shoulders even though their bellies are fat. Cows in fields look nicer from a distance.

Before I get to the edge of the field there's a small stream that has to be crossed. It's not deep but it's wide. There aren't any boulders to stand on. It's a waste of time taking my socks and shoes off. It only takes two and a bit big steps and I'm on the other side. My shoes look really clean when I shake the water off them. They won't stay like that although I wish they would.

The big house has a high hedge all the way round to the front. I climb over the gate at the corner of the field and follow the path round to the front of the house. A wooden sign says BRAEMAR. The main road is busy. There isn't a pavement to walk on, just a grass verge. The cars are alright but the lorries sound like an earthquake behind me. I get as near the hedge as possible. It's hard to tell how much further. The road winds up ahead. When the hedge stops and the wire fence begins, I crawl through to get back into the field.

I don't know what I'm going to say to Mr Shaugnessy. I'll tell him I'm sorry and I'll promise him I'll go back and try harder but what if he's in hospital or something worse has happened? They said my da wasn't well and then the next minute he was dead. And they had to tell me that because it was my da but they don't have to tell me anything about Mr Shaugnessy but they should because he likes me best out of everybody in the Homes and I help him the most. My throat feels tight and the grass blurs as the tears build up at the front of my eyes. If anything happens to Mr Shaugnessy I'm not going back to the Homes. I'll find out where Morag is and we'll both run away. We'll find out where Shuggy lives or see if Big Isa's still in West Street. They'd let us stay with them for a while. A church steeple and the roofs of some houses appear in the distance. That must be Kilmalcolm. My fingers start playing scales in my pockets. They do this all the time now, sometimes it's scales and sometimes it's passages from the pieces I'm learning. I can't stop them, then my head joins in and I can see the keys on the piano. Mostly it's OK and feels like an extra practice but sometimes it gets on my nerves and I tighten my hands into fists and think about something else until it goes away.

If Mr Shaugnessy's there he might go mad at me for turning up at his house. I might get him into trouble. It might make everything worse. Vera'll phone the duty social worker and they'll phone the police and tell them I was sent to bed for pestering the minister about Mr Shaugnessy and then I ran away and then they'll jump in their cars and go straight to Mr Shaugnessy's house and tell him what I've done. If there's a police car outside his house I'll keep away.

Kilmalcolm looks nice. The streets are clean and there are lots of trees along the sides of the road. I have to pass seventeen big houses before I get to the shops. Briarside Grange is the nicest. It has white walls and brown windows with matching, swirly curtains. The garden is mostly green with little clumps of blue and yellow flowers along the edges of the path. Two small statues of lions sit on either side of the steps leading up to the front door. My ma would love a house like this.

All the shops are closed except for the paper shop on my side of the street. The man inside is tying up newspapers into bundles and leaving them beside the door.

'S'cuse me, Mister, d'ye know where Woodlea Road is?'

The man looks up and finishes tying the string before he speaks. 'I do indeed, young lady; it's about four streets away on the other side of the road at the other end of the village. Who are you looking for?'

'Ma music teacher, Mr Shaugnessy. He lives on Woodlea Road.'

'Shaugnessy, Shaugnessy ... let me see now.' He goes behind the counter and takes out a big green book and starts flicking through the pages.

'You're absolutely right, young lady, he lives at number 47.' He looks at my legs and my shoes but I get out of the shop before he asks me any more questions.

Woodlea Road is on a small hill. The houses go up in steps and they all look the same; grey walls and brown doors. They're not as posh as the big houses at the other end. I can see Mr Shaugnessy's car on the left-hand side. There are no police cars around. Some kids are at the top of the street playing on bikes. A man on the other side of the street watches me while he washes his car. I walk up the steps to number 47. The nameplate on the door has a tartan pattern round the edges and a picture of purple heather either side of the name. Mr A. Shaugnessy.

I knock and step back onto the lower step. No one answers. There are no lights on but it's too early for lights. A vase of flowers stands in the middle of the window sill, the backs of two framed pictures sit either side. I bet it's his grandchildren. I knock again, this time a bit louder.

I can hear footsteps on stairs. Mr Shaugnessy opens the door. He looks the same but a little tired. I have to stop myself from putting my arms round his waist and squeezing him tight.

'Ailsa! My goodness. What on earth are you doing here?' He sticks his head out of the doorway and looks out onto the street. 'Did someone drop you off?'

'Ah walked it, Mr Shaugnessy.'

He looks at my shoes and socks and the mud on my legs. 'Goodness, gracious, Ailsa, you're soaked through.' He opens the door wider. 'Come in and get warm before you catch your death.' He gets me to take my shoes and socks off at the door and gives me his wife's brown furry slippers to put on. They've got zips at the front.

'Nobody would tell me where you were, Mr Shaugnessy, they kept saying it was none of my business so I just came to find out for myself.'

'Dearie me, you look like you've just stepped out of the trenches.' He smiles. 'Sit yourself down beside the fire and get warm, I'll stick the kettle on.' He goes into the kitchen.

I can hear the tap running and him sorting out cups and saucers and cupboard doors shutting and the fridge door closing. The fire is lovely. It's smaller than the one we had in Wallace Street but it's just as nice. The room isn't very big. A dark-green settee, with lacy mats on the arms and across the back, takes up the most room. The piano stands against the far wall. The pictures on the window sill are of his grandchildren, one on either side. His grand-daughter is wearing a dark-red school uniform with a blue shirt and a red-and-black-striped tie. Her teeth have gaps and they're different sizes. Mine are straight.

Mr Shaugnessy puts the tray down on the little table between the settee and the chair I'm sitting on. He's made some sandwiches and sliced up a sponge cake with icing on the top.

I sit forward in my chair. 'Ah'm sorry aboot the Academy, Mr Shaugnessy. Ah'm gonnay go back an work really hard.'

Mr Shaugnessy puts the teapot back on the tray. 'I can't say I wasn't disappointed, Ailsa, because I was.'

The lump quickly fills my throat. I put my head down and look at the carpet. I don't want him to see my eyes. The only sound in the room is the coals shifting in the grate.

'What you don't seem to understand, Ailsa, is you're just as good as the rest of the children at the Academy and, I'd wager, a better pianist than a fair few of them. They wouldn't have given you a place if you didn't deserve it, Ailsa. They have their reputation to think of.'

I swallow hard and cough as much of the tightness away as I can. 'The ear tests are really hard, Mr Shaugnessy, an this girl wi big eyebrows keeps lookin at me when ah canny get the answer an she keeps sayin she's rubbish but she's no ... her hand's up aw the time an she always gets her tests right an the rest ay them aw sit beside each other an they don't even speak tae ye ... they're aw posh nuts an they speak different tae me an they look different tae me.'

Mr Shaugnessy hands me a tissue. I wipe my eyes and my nose. I put my head in my hands to try and push back the pain at the front of my head. It feels like it's going to burst out through the bone and skin. Mr Shaugnessy gets up from the settee and sits on the arm of my chair.

'An Miss Ross only ever talks aboot the mistakes ye make an she never says the nice things that you dae an she disny care aboot ye ... it's in the door then oot again ...' He puts his arm across my shoulder and squeezes the top of my arm.

'Ah miss the music room an the cups a tea an ah miss you, Mr Shaugnessy, cos it's no the same as it wis before. When ah come up after school there's other people huvin their lessons an ah don't get tae see ye as much. Ah wish ah'd never gone tae the Academy.'

Mr Shaugnessy squeezes my arm a couple of times then hands me a cup of tea. He goes into the kitchen for something. I can hear him blowing his nose. The pain at the front of my head is almost gone. The tea tastes nice. Mr Shaugnessy sits back down on the settee.

'I miss you too, Ailsa. I miss you a great deal but when I feel sad about it I remind myself of why I don't see you as much and then I feel happy. You've moved on to better things although it might not feel like that to you.' He takes a few sips of his tea and hands me the plate of sandwiches, corned beef or cheese. I take the corned beef.

'I've spoken to your teacher at the Academy and she's very pleased with your progress. She thinks you're extremely talented but was understandably a bit confused as to why you stopped attending. I told her I'd speak to you and we'd sort it out.' He hands me the sandwich plate again. I take another corned beef.

'I'll give you extra help with the aural tests, Ailsa, we'll soon crack them, and although Miss Ross has a different style of teaching, she's one of the best pianists in the country. She even said she was already considering you for a performance at the end-of-year concert.' He gives me the look that says *so what do you make of that, eh?*

I didn't realise she liked me. I thought she couldn't be bothered with me. I smile at Mr Shaugnessy. He rocks back in his chair and claps his hands together. He puts a slice of cake onto a tea plate and places it on the table in front of me.

'Why huv ye been away, Mr Shaugnessy? Was it because ay whit ah did?'

Mr Shaugnessy shakes his head and smiles to himself. 'You get the daftest notions, Ailsa, it was nothing to do with you. My wife's just had a small operation and I took time off to be with her at the hospital. She'll be out in another day or two and I'll be back to work the week after next. As a matter of fact I was looking out some nighties for her upstairs when you knocked. I'll be popping up to the hospital shortly. I could drop you off on the way.'

I remember Vera. She's going to go mad. I don't care. She can still go and get fucked. If she starts with the punches and the slapping I'll just get stuck back into her. I'm not bothered about how many nights she sends me to bed early. Mr Shaugnessy and I are alright again.

67

The hall is filling up. The performers aren't allowed into the concert hall, we have to stay in the side room. You're allowed to open the door to the stage a little bit and have a look. Mr Shaugnessy is in the middle, in an aisle seat in the second row. His coat is folded across his knee and his hat sits on top. He's reading the programme very carefully.

Vera's sitting at one end of the front row and Sarah is at the other. They've brought the whole of Cottage 51 except for Mary and Shona; they're in Fintry, on a Girls' Brigade weekend. Ryan McCreedy swings his legs at the front. Vera pokes him on the knee. He doesn't look up. He just stops. He knows.

The other parents are still moving around, taking off jackets and putting bags on seats. They make a lot of noise.

'Mummy's found us a lovely seat, Myrtle, so we can watch Philip play his clarinet.' Myrtle's not listening. She's running between the rows of chairs. Her skirt looks too long for her and she's wearing a red baggy jumper. She looks about seven but she's still got a dummy, it's attached to a ribbon round her neck, like a medal.

'Myrtle darling, Mummy's got some lovely raisins to give you.' Myrtle is trying to climb onto the stage. Vera glares at her and looks at Sarah.

The violinist stands closely behind me, on tiptoe so that he can see into the hall. I move back into the room to let him have a proper look. Miss Ross walks towards me smiling.

'Nervous?' I nod my head. 'You'll be fine. Remember the con brio starts off piano but make sure you attack the right hand and don't let the broken octaves overpower everything.' I nod. 'And the rests in the opening bars are just as important as the notes.' I nod again. 'You'll be wonderful, Ailsa, enjoy it.'

My arms feel funny, like they've lost all their strength, but they always feel like that before piano exams and once you start playing they go back to normal. Miss Ross told me she still gets nervous before a performance so she has to sit away from everyone else, put her hands in her lap, close her eyes and think about her favourite place. She said it works, if you really concentrate. Miss Ross doesn't look like she'd get nervous about anything.

The man from the auditions wishes us all good luck and walks out onto the stage. The hall goes quiet. Six of us are performing. I'm fourth. The waiting room is quiet while the performances take place, apart from the blowing sounds into instruments to keep them warm. I find a seat in the corner, place my music on the seat beside me and let my arms and hands fall as loosely as they can into my lap. I close my eyes and I'm in the music room. Mr Shaugnessy is sitting at his desk, surrounded by music and manuscript paper. He doesn't see me. He is busy writing out parts for the choir. Sunlight doesn't reach the corners but fills the rest of the room.

The smells of old books and dust and resin feel familiar. I breathe them in. I swallow all the sounds of the room, the music, the laughter, the stories, the advice. My shoe gently rubs against the worn bit of carpet nearest the piano. I'm part of the reason why it's worn and faded. I'm part of the piano and the instruments and all the handles of all the drawers and cupboard doors. I'm in the walls and window sills and the velvet-topped piano stool. I'm in the notes I copied onto papers that lie in folders, waiting to be played. I am . . .

'Ailsa, you're up next.' Miss Ross finds the page in my music book. 'Did it work?' She looks at me, smiling.

'I think so.' My arms feel back to normal.

'Good stuff. C'mon then.'

The hall isn't packed but it's pretty full. I bow and give Mr Shaugnessy a smile. His clapping is louder than everyone else's. As I play the opening C minor chord I think of Ryan McCreedy. He's going to be sick to the back teeth of this tune. I dot the rhythms as short as I can and give the rests their full value. The descending chromatic scale pauses on an A flat before the Allegro di molto e con brio section. I prepare myself for the speed of it. In my head it's fast but steady. My fingers don't listen to my head. They fly across the piano from the very first note. It's like they're laughing at me, saying c'mon then, catch us if you can. After I get over the initial shock of what they're doing, I concentrate like mad to keep them under control. I pull it back a fraction at the right-hand crossover melody but not enough to spoil the energy of it.

Part of me is terrified of it all rushing in on itself to a crash but another part of me loves it. It's taken on a life of its own and even though it's going at a tremendous lick I'm still able to make a difference between the sforzandos and the fortes and the pianos. The return of the subject gives me a chance to catch my breath. I'll have to maintain the tempo I started with but at least this time I'm ready for it.

Mr Shaugnessy is already on his feet as I play the last C minor chord. The audience clap and smile as I bow. My legs don't feel like they're working properly as I make my way off the stage.

'Ashkenazy would have had trouble keeping up with

you there, Ailsa.' Miss Ross lets the breath out of her mouth and puts her arm round my shoulder. 'My heart was in my mouth the whole time. I thought, she's never going to make it.'

I smile. I'm relieved and happy. 'Mr Shaugnessy stood up at the end, did you see him?'

She nods her head. 'He looks like he's fit to burst, Ailsa. He's really proud.'

The last two performers play well. The man from the auditions gets up on stage to say a few words at the end and makes us all come back on stage for one last bow. Mr Shaugnessy's back on his feet. His jaw must be aching with all the smiling he's doing. When the applause dies down we're allowed to leave the stage and join the audience.

Mr Shaugnessy hugs me tight for ages. 'What a performance, Ailsa! You were absolutely tremendous, cool as a cucumber and you looked so professional.' I can't get a word in edgeways. 'What a polished performance and beautiful expression and articulation ...'

Vera looms with the rest of the cottage.

Ryan McCreedy pushes himself to the front. 'Ye were really good, Ailsa – yer fingers were goin really fast.'

I smile at him and stroke the back of his head.

'The minibus is waiting outside, Mr Shaugnessy, we'll have to get Ailsa home.' She doesn't smile. She wants me to move straight away but I haven't said goodbye to Miss Ross.

'Well, if you don't mind, Miss Chambers, Ailsa's teacher and I are going to take her out for a special tea, y'know, to celebrate. Wasn't she wonderful?'

Vera smiles that small smile of hers when she's trying to make out she's not bothered but she is.

'I'll drop her off on my way home, Miss Chambers. We'll not keep her out too late.'

I give Ryan a wave as he follows Vera out of the hall.

I've just turned thirteen. I've just given a really good performance at the Royal Scottish Academy of Music and Drama and I'm just as good as anybody else.

Afterword

I stood at the graveside. I was one of about two hundred. I knew the minister was at the front of the crowd, doing the whole we commit this body to the ground thing, but I couldn't really hear him. It didn't matter, it helped just to stand quietly and remember him. An ice-cream van jangled 'Summer Holiday' in the distance. An old woman in front of me turned and scowled in the direction of the sound.

I felt as if I should have been up at the front, just behind his family. I didn't like being at the back. I didn't like sharing him with all those other people. I imagined the crowds parting, once they realised who I was and what we had meant to each other.

A sound from the front of the crowd built until it reached the back, as more and more voices joined in. 'When the Roll is Called up Yonder'. My mouth moved but the sounds couldn't get past the hard fist of pain in my throat. The singing fell into four-part harmony. It was perfect. Mr Shaugnessy would have liked it. It reminded me of the Mission Hall in Greenock.

When the singing stopped, the minister said something else but he was too far away for the sound to carry properly. I prayed hard that Mr Shaugnessy was right about the God he had so much faith in. I prayed hard that his God was looking after him. I pictured him in the whitest, most comfortable of robes, sitting at God's right hand, smiling that smile of his.

The mourners started to scatter. They walked slowly, heads down. Their team had lost. They made their way back to the main hall at the Homes for tea and sandwiches.

It wasn't like my mother's funeral, eight years earlier. Hers was very small; a quiet, bemusing affair. I hadn't been able to work out what I was supposed to feel. I'd wanted Morag to be there; she'd tried but she hadn't been able to make it.

The main hall hadn't changed; the same curtains covered the front of the stage, the piano still sat in the corner. I checked the gallery for ghosts.

I scanned the faces in the crowd for Vera. I recognised a few house-parents but she wasn't amongst them. She'd left to get married and I hadn't seen her since. Who'd be Vera, eh? Who'd want her head and her conscience?

Mr Shaugnessy's son stood in front of me. He held out his hand.

'Thank you for coming,' he said. He was Mr Shaugnessy's double. It was comforting to look at him.

'Ailsa Dunn,' I told him. 'I used to live here and Mr Shaugnessy taught me piano.' I shook his hand.

'Oh *you're* Ailsa Dunn,' he said and started smiling and nodding his head. 'Dad often talked about you and how talented you were.'

It was like some sort of floodgate had opened. My hands couldn't wipe away the tears fast enough. I scratted around in my pockets for a hankie. He rubbed the side of my arm and let me get myself together.

'So what are you doing with yourself now, Ailsa?' he asked.

I coughed the feelings out of my throat. 'I'm Head of Music at a school in Newcastle.' I cleared my throat again.

'My oh my,' he said. He smiled like Mr Shaugnessy; his eyes went big in the same way. 'And did Dad know you'd made a career for yourself in music?'

I wiped at my nose with the hankie and nodded. 'We kept in touch. He sent me old recordings of his favourite pieces I'd played; from grade one, right through to grade eight.'

He nodded as I spoke.

'I listened to them more for the introductions. *Ailsa will now play . . .* He'd give you the composer, the opus number if it had one, the day, the date and the year.'

His son laughed and clasped his hands together. 'That sounds like Dad.'

We looked at each other and I could tell he understood how important his father had been to me.

Before leaving the Homes, I drove around the familiar paths and avenues. The grounds were beautiful. I took the long way to the main gate, past Cottage 51. I slowed down but I didn't stop. I filled the front seat with tape after tape from the glove compartment until I found one: 'Ailsa Dunn (1974) piano solos and Trinity College Exam pieces'. The tape hissed in the silence. *Ailsa will now play . . .*

Acknowledgements

I love the acknowledgements page. I love to look for clues about the writer, find out a bit more about the process they've gone through, and I feel slightly cheated when it's just a list of names that mean nothing to me but everything to the people mentioned. I like acknowledgements with details, especially when the author is specific about the ways in which people have helped. Needless to say, I do not intend to short-change the reader or my friends in this, the best of all possible tasks.

Huge thanks to Sheila Mulhern for her support and encouragement from the get-go and her regular invitations to perform at the Blue Room in Newcastle.

Deepest thanks to James Welsh, Paul Bodie, Isabel Garford and Chris Algar for being part of the Mark Toney writing group which knocked the majority of the memoir into shape. Their suggestions and observations were second to none and developed my writing immeasurably. Particular thanks to Chris Algar for the use of her cottage in Marske-by-the-Sea to complete the book. I'm indebted.

Special thanks to my two best friends, Isabel Garford and Geoff Weston, for their unwavering support and friendship and not allowing me to give up when I all but had. And an extra thank you to Geoff for the very flattering author photograph.

Special thanks to Margaret Wilkinson, a tutor par excellence.

Particular thanks to Marion Urch at Adventures in Fiction. The mentoring was invaluable, but more importantly the validation as a writer was priceless.

A big thank you to my sister Moira who made me read extracts to her over the phone, who laughed at all the right bits and went quiet when it got to the sad bits.

Huge thanks to everyone at HHB Literary Agency, especially Elly James, who championed this book from the start and worked tirelessly to help me get it into the best possible shape for submission. She is a truly impressive young woman and I'm a huge fan of hers.

Finally, thanks to Alexandra Pringle and everyone at Bloomsbury – Alexa von Hirschberg, Katie Bond, Sue Pearse, Adrian Downie, Holly Macdonald, Emma Daley, Trâm-Anh Doan – for making me feel so welcome and appreciated. In particular, heartfelt thanks to Anna Simpson for her meticulous, sympathetic editing.

A Note on the Type

The text of this book is set in Adobe Caslon, named after the English punch-cutter and type-founder William Caslon I (1692–1766). Caslon's rather old-fashioned types were modelled on seventeenth-century Dutch designs, but found wide acceptance throughout the English-speaking world for much of the eighteenth century until being replaced by newer types towards the end of the century. Used in 1776 to print the Declaration of Independence, they were revived in the nineteenth century, and have been popular ever since, particularly amongst fine printers. There are several digital versions, of which Carol Twombly's Adobe Caslon is one.